CLERICAL E
A VICTORIAN SERIES
VOLUME 2

By

TOM HUGHES

Copyright 2017 by Tom Hughes

All Rights Reserved

Squeaking Chair Books

www.victorianga@aol.com

PREFACE TO VOLUME TWO

"OF CLERICAL SCANDALS
THERE SEEM NO END."[1]

When Victoria took the throne in 1837 and assumed, among many, the title of Defender of the Faith, there were about 14,000 clergymen employed in the Church of England. By her death, 64 years later, that number had more than doubled. From the grandest episcopal palace to the remotest rectory, almost without exception, these men lived and died in service to their Church and congregation. Temporally, they avoided notoriety. They broke no laws. They married happily and raised their young. They held fetes and cream teas. Many wrote books - sacred and secular. Some grew roses, studied spiders or kept bees. Their earthly reward generally has been a one-line mention inscribed upon the "roll of vicars" (rectors, curates, priests-in-charge, as applicable) affixed to a side wall of their church, a list in many cases dating back centuries. This is by way of making plain that notwithstanding that a second volume has been published and a third is in the early stages of preparation, the numbers of misconducting clerics was actually quite small. Still, for those who delight in a good vicarage scandal, the Victorian church offered an "unpleasantly abundant crop."[2]

When one of this fraction of miscreants found himself sideways before the public, the sensation was immediate. Headline writers delighted in detailing the singular, remarkable, extraordinary, disgraceful, outrageous and/or heartless conduct of any clergyman. *Reynolds' Newspaper*, a radical journal and quite anti-clerical, declared in 1870, "Clerical scandals have of late grown as rife as those peculiar scandals which pre-eminently affect high society."[3] But profligacy amongst the peerage was almost to be expected. The clergy were presumed to be exemplars of morality. Thus, "Of all the scandals that come under the consideration of newspaper readers, a clerical scandal is the most deplorable. Sinners that we are, we instinctively expect something better from the gentlemen who undertake to teach us the way."[4] Matthew Parris, author of *The Great Unfrocked*, believes the public's deep and continuing interest in these stories has ever been "pure *schadenfreude.*"[5]

While offering diverting amusement to the enemies of the established religion and lining the pockets of the newspaper publishers, these controversies meant staggering costs to the church itself. In the case of Mr. Karr (see Chapter 5), the parade of litigation cost the diocese of Gloucester a huge fortune. Protected by arcane ecclesiastical law and excellent legal representation, many a troublesome cleric could defy efforts to remove him. It was not until 1893, that a new Clergy Discipline Act cleared Parliament with the intent of empowering the Church and stream-lining the process. Parson Young's lark in London (see Chapter 1) would be one of the act's more prominent early tests.

The five anecdotal accounts herein were selected from the author's unique database, numbering hundreds of Victorian clergymen. For more details, see the acknowledgements.

Parson Young's Night Out - a boisterous Yorkshireman finds himself rector of a posh parish in a quiet Surrey village. The Rev. Charles Gordon Young was initially popular in the pulpit and on the cricket ground. His critics, however, suspected the rector drank too much. What were the local "swells" of Chipstead to think when their clergyman was found in a notorious London club with a lady of the evening upon his knee?

A Case of Heartless Villainy - His prospects blighted, his health ruined, the Rev. Richard Marsh Watson made a living in a clerical agency and selling sermons. And a bit of blackmail. Having seduced his wife's sister, Watson required her to purchase his silence. When she, at last, refused to pay, the ensuing trial shocked all Britain. Still, as one newspaper wondered, "What are we to think of the young women who yielded to the advances of a scrofulous parson with one leg?"

A Clerical Lothario - The Rev. Turberville Cory-Thomas, complimented frequently on his "dagger moustache," was quite popular with the church ladies in the rapidly growing parish of Acton Green in West London. His vicar praised him regularly. Until, that is, Mr. Cory-Thomas was accused of attempting to seduce two sisters - one over lunch at Gatti's, the other in a grim bedsit near Euston Station. The ensuing slander trial shared the front pages with news of Queen Victoria's death.

I'll Do for Dicky Rodgers - A summer outing on the Broads was under the charge of the Rev. Edward Rodgers, curate of Lowestoft. Too much sun, too much smoke and drink at the "after-party" in the pub, and Rodgers was poorly. A local youth offered to help him home. What happened in the darkened lane between the hedgerows? George Rix began telling everyone, "He must have thought I was his wife."

The Irreproachable Mr. Karr - Handsome, sporting and the darling of the raffish set at Berkeley Castle was the Rev. John Seton Karr. In the town, however, the vicar's suavity may have gone too far. Was Mr. Karr's gift of satin dancing shoes to a local solicitor's wife in any way appropriate? But when Mrs. Gaisford, known for her extraordinary teeth, called upon Mr. Karr at his London hotel, sensational rumours were aroused leading to a series of legal battles that, literally, worried a Bishop to death.

TABLE OF CONTENTS

Preface

1. Parson Young's Night Out   7
Rev. Charles Gordon Young, Rector of Chipstead, Surrey

2. A Case of Heartless Villainy   53
Rev. Richard Marsh Watson, Clerk in Holy Orders

3. A Clerical Lothario   81
Rev. Turberville Cory-Thomas, Curate of St. Alban's, Acton Green, London

4. I'll Do for Dicky Rodgers   119
Rev. Edward Rodgers, Curate of Lowestoft, Suffolk

5. The Irreproachable Mr. Karr   151
Rev. John Seton Karr, Vicar of Berkeley, Gloucestershire

Acknowledgements

Endnotes

1. PARSON YOUNG'S NIGHT OUT

REV. CHARLES G. YOUNG.

Is it possible that a constitutional change has taken place in the Clergy of the present day, or that the wine they drink is of so inferior a quality that it affects their heads more readily than the generous liquor imbibed by their predecessors? Clergymen in former years were in the habit of drinking port wine by the bottle without apparently suffering any ill effects. The whole question is shrouded in mystery.[6]

19 November 1901

The Chapter House in Southwark was nearly empty. A sentence of deprivation was rarely imposed in the Church of England. Mr. Dibdin, chancellor of the Diocese of Rochester, read aloud the verdict that had been reached after several lengthy days of testimony in a Consistory Court. The Rev. Charles Gordon Young, rector of Chipstead, Surrey, had been found guilty of repeated instances of drunkenness. Most sensationally, however, he was found to have been in a night-club, frequented by immoral men and women, with a prostitute perched upon his knee. In sum, these were actions unworthy of the character of a minister of religion. The chancellor had made his decision but only a bishop could pronounce deprivation. The Rt. Rev Edward Talbot[7], the Bishop of Rochester, rose, wearing the full purple robes of his office. His voice reverberated about the empty galleries. Listeners detected his voice catching as he spoke:

> It is a most painful thing to be called upon to condemn a brother in the ministry of God. I can only pray—and I earnestly pray—that this grievous pain may not only be for the honour of God and the purity of His Church, and for the good of the people of the parish of Chipstead, but also be for him upon whom it passes the means of amendment

and recovery that he may be restored by God's grace to the exercise of his ministry in the Church of God.

Benediction followed. The Rev. Mr. Young was not in attendance.

* * * * *

St. Margaret's Chipstead (2016)

Not fifteen miles from Charing Cross lies the idyllic Surrey village of Chipstead.

> No high road goes thru the village, if the collection of cottages by the church can be dignified by that name. All is peaceful. The rooks are busy in the elm branches, and in the proper season cuckoo answers to cuckoo. The nightingale is not heard merely

in the stillness of the night, but in broad day all round, mingled with the musical ring of the village blacksmith's anvil.[8]

It is still true today that no high road passes through the village; the M25 to the south and A23 to the east are just far enough away. The evocative excerpt quoted above comes from the annual report of the Ecclesiological Society for 1890. Touring Surrey churches that year, their representatives came to Chipstead to inspect St. Margaret's, an ancient flint church that sits on a lofty eminence of just over 500-feet, thereby commanding outstanding views. After much discussion of clerestories, piscinas and quatrefoils, the Society declared to its members that Chipstead church was "worth a special visit."

No mention was made in the society's otherwise thorough report on Chipstead church of the new rector, the Rev. Charles Gordon Young. He had come to the village in late 1888, succeeding the Rev. Peter Aubertin, who resigned owing to ill-health. Aubertins, father and then son, had been rectors in Chipstead for almost seventy years. Of the Rev. Peter the younger, they wrote:
> A delight in the country and in country pursuits, the deceased was a quiet influence for good, and his purse was always at the service of distressed parishioners.[9]

This was going to be a very tough act to follow for the new rector.

The Rev. Mr. Young was born in 1861 in Oughtibridge, a Yorkshire village northwest of Sheffield. His father had risen from making bricks to become a mining engineer but the family had relocated to south London by the 1870's. Living in Camberwell, at 20, Charles was employed in the surveyor of taxes office. He felt called to the Church of England ministry and in 1883 he entered the London College of Divinity in Highbury. Twas a grand name but the school was relatively new, a small privately funded venture, dedicated to teaching an evangelical strain of Anglicanism. The greater number of their students were older men who'd come to the clergy from the trades.

Young was ordained in 1886 and, as did most of the LCD graduates, he eschewed a bosky parish for an urban pulpit. He was licensed to be a curate for the Rev. Sidney Bott, vicar of St. Jude's church serving London's new Queen's Park Housing Estate. He arrived with his new wife, Mary Bishop, a printer's daughter from Camberwell. Marriage was not recommended for curates: the pay was meagre, job security nil. Still, Young made a lasting contribution in the parish. He's remembered for helping to found the Queens Park Rangers, the local football club that remains a fixture in the English game today.[10] That's not germane to our larger story but what is was the fact that Rev. Young and his vicar fell out and the young curate's stay in Queen's Park was not long. At first, all Young could find was a post as chaplain at the St. Marylebone Infirmary in Ladbroke Grove. He hated it.

In 1887, a great deal of work was being done to improve the London-Brighton railway line. Young found himself in Surrey ministering to the railway navvies in Merstham. The new station there was only two miles from Chipstead. The clergymen in the area took favourable notice of the charismatic newcomer. In December 1888, Chipstead rectory came open. The "living" of Chipstead was controlled by the Jolliffe family – then represented by the 2d Baron Hylton, a survivor of the Charge of the Light Brigade. Just before Christmas, the Bishop of Rochester, in whose diocese was to be found Chipstead, announced that the Baron was pleased to present the rectory to the Rev. Charles Gordon Young. The living was valued at just £430 per year so, despite the fine setting, it was not the most sought after rectory in the land. This might help explain the rather curious choice of the Rev. Young.

The skills learned and techniques applicable to a navvy congregation might not be easily transferable to a quiet church in what was, even then, part of the affluent stockbroker belt around the capital. The Aubertins, descended from a wealthy Huguenot merchant family, were very comfortable amongst their own kind. The new rector, a Yorkshireman no less, was a different kind of clergyman for Chipstead. Everyone, even his admirers, would say that Young was loud and excitable. Emotions came easy for him, too easy, perhaps. He was given to back-slapping, joke-telling and a general heartiness that some found appealing while others thought dubious attributes for a clergyman.

People often do confound expectations. The Rev. Young proved himself to be quite a popular fellow both in the pulpit and on the playing fields. Congregations increased at St. Margaret's. The Harvest Festival service was "excessively crowded." A fundraising campaign was begun for long needed repairs to the twelfth century church. To signal his approval, the (aforementioned) Bishop Talbot came down from Rochester, the first prelate to visit Chipstead in 35 years. At a garden party at the rectory, surrounded by the local gentry, Talbot thanked Young for his service. "What a contrast it is to come down out of the streets of South London to the hills of Surrey and to believe we are all part of one great organisation trying to do particular work."

Certainly a day to be remembered for the Rev. Mr. Young. But, as he cheerfully insisted at the Chipstead cricket team's annual dinner in 1893, being rector was fine but he was more proud to be captain of the local eleven. Cricket played a unique role in late-Victorian village life:

> The Village Cricket Club is an institution which, when properly managed, does more good in a parish towards establishing friendly relations between classes than all the Friendly Societies put together, or even a course of sermons on brotherly kindness.[11]

Cricket, not football, was the game in Chipstead and Mr. Young was made captain in 1891. Given his reputation, Young seems a bold choice as the experts thought a captain should have a calm head. "The nervous and excitable class is perhaps the worst of all ... continually rushing about, altering the field without any reason, shouting excitedly at the top of his voice whenever a fielder has to stop or throw up the ball, and generally creating a feeling of uneasiness and excitement among players and spectators.[12]" The village side played XI's from around Surrey. Young's name was frequently seen in the agate box scores. In 1893, he played well in a match versus the Cane Hill Lunatic Asylum (physicians and staff only.) To keep fresh, the Chipstead club would be divided up and "friendly" village matches played. Mr. Young's XI, for instance, vanquished Mr. Rucker's XI, the latter gentleman residing at Reeves Rest, one of the fine estates in Chipstead. The matches were played on grounds donated by John Cattley of Shabden Park, the finest of them all.

Mr. Young's influence expanded beyond the village, as well. He was elected to the Reigate Board of Guardians, administering the "poor laws," and the Reigate Rural District Council, which dealt with sundry local issues. He was a regular advocate for maintaining the public footpaths and improving the roads, a personal cause as he had been thrown from his bicycle on more than one occasion.

So, what was the problem? Why is he included in this collection? For most of his first decade in

Chipstead, the Rev. Young had few problems with his flock. By the late 1890's, however, a growing number of Chipstead residents had concluded that their exuberant rector was too often drunk. But there are always two sides to a story. When the Chipstead scandal broke, the *Daily Mail,* then as now, given to hyperbole, declared: "Never was a little village so divided."

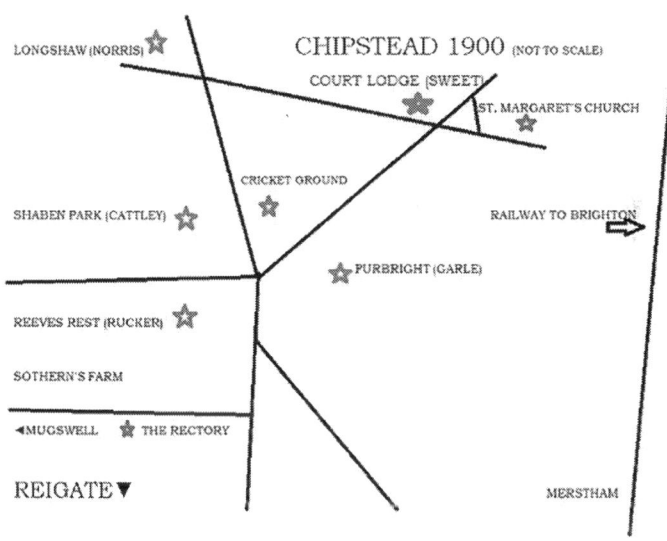

Topographically, there was a Chipstead "village." St. Margaret's, however, dating from the 12th century, was "unusually" sited some distance to the south and east. The sizeable rectory, of more recent vintage, was an additional five minute cycle ride away in an area known as Mugswell. This was a place of "much pleasant scenery" built over with several larger estates and homes. It was here that the events of the Young scandal unfolded.[13]

One of the estates, Purbright House, a "substantial" 17th century manor, was the home of John Acton Garle, who managed a gold mining syndicate on the London exchange. He owned the first phonograph in Chipstead which he had graciously loaned for use at one of Mr. Young's fund-raisers. Perhaps to repay that gesture, the Youngs invited Garle to dine at the rectory in March 1897. After the meal, as Mrs. Young saw to things in the kitchen, Amy Mings, the housemaid brought in the dessert dishes. Garle fancied himself to be something of an artist and there had been much talk of painting during dinner. As the young lady set the table, Garle was shocked to hear the rector make some rather inappropriate comments on her "fine form." Young went on, saying, "Wouldn't she make a fine model? Wouldn't you like to see her stripped?" Garle was stunned, thinking the rector had drunk too much port. He left soon thereafter but told no one.

Later that year, in November, Reginald Rucker, a metals merchant in the City, residing at Reeves Rest, hosted a shooting party followed by dinner and drinks for the men and their wives. Rucker was in his 40's, married, and knew the rector from the cricket club and the parish council. Rucker recalled that Mr. Young arrived after dinner when the ladies had gone into the drawing room. He seemed rather boisterous and confided to his host that he had already had a glass or two of port. Young quickly downed a glass of whisky and began talking a lot of "awful rubbish." Rucker suggested they all rejoin the ladies, but paused to make the rector "a thundering weak" whisky. Young was known to be a vivacious chap and usually made for good company but on this evening, with the ladies, he began telling a rather ribald story about a maidservant at a pub who had to give an old man a bath. Rucker finally interrupted the rector to say, "Steady, Young," and he contrived to get the man out of such mixed company. Young seemed to understand that he had embarrassed his host and began, in the most maudlin manner, to apologise. The Ruckers had been so good to him, etc., etc. Young shook Rucker's hand a half-dozen times before departing.

The rectory was a good footpath's walk away and Young's return home was to be made even longer when he came upon a locked gate at Sothern's Farm. Now, this was another sore point with him, and seeing lights in the stables, he proceeded directly to confront the groom, William Bale. The lad had no knowledge why the gate was locked but seeing how unsteady the rector seemed to be, he gave him a lantern. Bale claimed to then watch the clergyman storm off into the darkness, walking directly into a pond. That story got around quickly and Mr. Rucker soon heard of it. A few days later, he wrote a note to Young urging the rector to moderate his drinking or even consider taking the pledge. He received a polite letter in return; the rector thanked him for his interest.

These were certainly a couple of amusing anecdotes for village gossip. Remember, "The rector drinks a little," was far from an uncommon situation. But around Chipstead, these incidents simply added to a growing list. The rector snickered his way through an entire scripture reading. At choir practice, he behaved in an extraordinary fashion, bellowing at the boys and threatening to fight Prothero, the organist. Mr. Young seemed exceedingly accident prone: he was thrown from his trap and took repeated spills from his cycle. Even on the cricket ground – on one memorable day - Young was shouting and carrying on to such an extent he found himself completely out of position, in front of the wickets, and accidentally kicked them down. He later completely collapsed to the ground.

There had been several efforts by Rucker and others to address the issue with Mr. Young. During one meeting, when it was suggested that he take a two-year leave of absence, the rector threw himself on to the floor, crying, "I am ruined!" He made protestations of impending reform. In 1899, on the advice of his wife and some friends, the rector decided to take some time off. He went alone, booking passage on a "health & pleasure cruise" for Morocco, with stops at various islands and watering places along the way. In Morocco, he went inland to see the famous Atlas Mountains. Among the traveling party was a young Cambridge man, Cecil Spearing[14], whose older brother was a clergyman. Everyone was advised not to drink the water in Morocco - Young stuck with brandy - but Spearing became dangerously ill. Young remained with the fellow until he was strong enough to return to England. They landed at Gravesend on 3 July 1899. Oxford and Cambridge were to play their annual varsity cricket match at Lord's the next day. All the university sporting types would come up to town for a good time. Spearing, wishing to thank Young, invited him to join his little party for supper at the Hotel Continental. Varsity Day passed well into varsity night. It was past midnight, with most everything closed in London, when Spearing suggested they move on to the Alsatian Club.

Presumably a clergyman would not have heard of this establishment at 72 New Oxford Street, although a recent police raid had been in all the papers.[15] The ground floor featured a small bar. There was also "a smaller room where a perfectly horrible supper was served for an outrageous price."[16] The first floor was lavishly decorated with plush red walls, divans and banquettes surrounding a highly-polished dance floor and a small area for the musicians. The Alsatian was a private club for gentlemen but women of a certain profession were admitted as well. Having paid his guinea to become a "member," Young and his younger companions, eschewing the pricy food, climbed the stairs to the club. The others soon drifted away; the rector of Chipstead, in his clerical suit and collar, was sitting alone. One of the ladies, in a white evening gown of impressive décolletage, took pity and offered to sit on his knee, a proposal to which he did not object. It was at that very moment that three new gentleman arrived at the Alsatian. That these three young men, parishioners of St. Margaret's, could have walked in to this particular nightclub on this particular evening to find their rector in situ with a dubious woman perched on his knee has to be one of the more bizarre coincidences ever recorded. Or was it? More speculation to follow.

Who were these newcomers? Wentworth Ewing was the designated heir to Chipstead's magnificent Shabden Park. Everyone called him "Wentie." With him on this visit to the Alsatian were his younger brother, Guy Ewing, and Henry Butler, who had just inherited his father's wine business. The Butlers lived at Elmore in Chipstead. The three men approached Young with the quite sensible question of "What are you doing here?" The young lady, to her great credit, patted the clergyman's cheek and kindly cooed, "He's a poor dear." She gave up her comfortable position and decamped, bidding the small, awkward party a good night. Guy Ewing, the youngest in the group, began chaffing the rector, calling him a "naughty boy," and went so far as to publicly administer a mock spanking. Young explained that he had never been there before and had only come with some friends – who were then lost in the merry-making masses around them. But he was delighted to see such friendly faces from Chipstead as he was just getting ready to leave.

Given all this background, it is hard to fathom why it was another full year after the Alsatian confrontation before the first significant effort was made to remove Young from the Chipstead pulpit.

By 1900, the Youngs had decided to "let" the rectory to a tenant and they moved into rooms at April Cottage, home of the Richbell family in Mugswell[17]. On Sunday, 29 July 1900, the Rev. Mr. Young – blaming his landlady's clock for the mix-up - arrived late for the services. But his readings were quite slurred. On 3 August, the rector received the following letter:

> We the undersigned, members of the parish of Chipstead, feel that in view of your continued insobriety, in spite of promises to amend, it has become most desirable in the interests of the parish, and your own interests, that you should make a fresh start elsewhere. We hope that in new surroundings you may be able to exercise influence for good, which it is impossible to be exercised any longer by you in this parish.

The signers included Messrs. Wentworth E. Cattley[18], R.W. Rucker, J.A. Garle, Frank Goad (who had replaced the rector as captain of the cricket club) and Arthur Norris. The Norrises, who lived at the Longshaw estate, were particular friends of Mrs. Young and their daughter had stayed with the Youngs on many occasions. The letter ended with a muted warning that this "unpleasant situation ... cannot be prolonged indefinitely."

The letter to the rector was drafted by Charles Sweet, a solicitor in Lincoln's Inn Fields. A fastidious bachelor whose London address was the posh Albany in Piccadilly, Sweet was relatively new in the village, residing at Court Lodge Cottage, quite near the church. In addition to the formal letter, Sweet wrote privately to the rector, urging him to seek an exchange with another clergyman, thus avoiding a public scandal. Young answered with explanations for all the reported occasions of drink. The correspondence ended in hostility. Sweet writing: "You do not care to answer? I am not surprised." In October, the rector admitted to having struggled with drink and promised to take the pledge. "I admit that I have been greatly to blame, but I trust that my unfortunate and well-known excitability of temperament will be taken into consideration." He may have been too late, however. Mr. Young was informed that nine in ten in Chipstead wanted him gone. In December 1900, the Rev. and Mrs. Young left Chipstead. A curate-in-charge was assigned to the parish.

Quiet was never an attribute applied to Young and he would not go quietly either. He would vigorously contest the charges against him, contending that he was the victim of a village cabal hatched among "the moneyed classes." The story of the "vivacious rector and his parish" was to be aired before a Consistory Court in London. The case would be tried under the relatively new Clergy Discipline Act of 1892, described as a "cheap and expeditious" way of removing so-called "criminous clerics." The Chipstead affair would prove to be neither cheap nor anything near to expeditiously resolved. Public drunkenness was a removable offense under the new act and, on that score, Young was facing all of sixteen counts! Additionally, for his visit to the

Alsatian club, he was charged with behaving in an "immoral and riotous manner" with prostitutes.

One might well ask why so much was made of a rector occasionally in his cups? Alcoholism among the clergy was a serious problem. "Many a lonely or disillusioned parson turned to drink."[19] During the debate on the new discipline act, some argued that only public drunkenness should be actionable, let the poor man drink at home. Even a clergyman with the best intentions, in a social village such as Chipstead, was regularly tempted.

> On all manner of occasions—if it be at a baptism, a marriage, or a funeral ...
> whatever else may be produced, the Bottle is sure to be called forth and he makes himself conspicuous who dares refuse to drink "the genial glass."[20]

But drunken clerics who missed their services, embarrassed their congregations from the pulpit, fell into newly dug graves at a funeral or beat their wives and children were an undoubted scandal to the church. That said, did the Rev. Mr. Young's alleged failings rise to any of that?

The proceedings began on Saturday, 19 October 1901. Owing to the number of witnesses and the interest the case had generated, it was decided to hold the trial in the Law Courts in the Strand. "The peaceful little Surrey village of Chipstead put on its best clothes on Saturday and migrated to London," recorded the *Daily Mail*. The immensity of the splendid Central Hall, with its vaulted 80-foot ceiling, had the "yokels gaping with astonishment." The public gallery space in Courtroom III was quickly filled; the Chipstead ladies "primly fluttered" their skirts to be comfortably seated. Mrs. Young was present, seated with the Rev. A.G. Rogers from the village of Gatton, near Chipstead. Her husband sat at the defence table, "clean-shaven, alert and determined" alongside his lead counsel, John Rawlinson. Presiding over all of this was Lewis Dibdin, chancellor of the Diocese of Rochester. Five "assessors" would act as a jury – two prominent laymen and three clergyman, all from the diocese.

The promoter's case - or the prosecution - was in the hands of Charles Gill. The still young Irish-born barrister had already appeared in many sensational cases. His chambers in the Temple were hung with "a series of prints and drawings illustrating [his] many memorable trials." Gill spoke for two hours, detailing the "scandalous" events of the previous five years that had brought them to that day, one everyone in Chipstead had hoped to avoid. Many of the witnesses to be heard had long been intimate friends of the Rev. and Mrs. Young. Many good people had urged the rector to moderate his drinking, he refused. They pleaded with him to take the pledge. He refused. To avoid scandal, they entreated him to exchange his living but he would not do it. Instead, Mr. Young presented denials and excuses: he was excitable, he was over-emotional, he had an old injury that made him walk unsteadily, he forgot to wind his clock, the pulpit steps were uneven, the roads were bad, hence his many cycling mishaps. But the people of Chipstead had had enough of their rector and his flask. Mention of the flask prompted some tutt-ing and tsk-ing from the gallery that was quickly hushed. Gill called Mr. Reginald Rucker to the stand.

NB: The witnesses - for and against - testified over three days. For reasons of availability or strategy, there was no chronological sequence of testimony. For narrative convenience, there will be. The evidence will be grouped under three headings: general drunkenness, the cricket field incident and the Alsatian club.

Reeves Rest, 2016

Mr. Rucker recounted the evening at his home, Reeves Rest, in late 1897 when Mr. Young's bawdy anecdote had so upset the drawing room ladies. Mr. Rawlinson, finally getting to speak in the matter, cross-examined the witness. If the rector had arrived in an excited condition, why had Rucker immediately poured him a large whisky? If Young was talking "awful rubbish," why did the witness think it was a good idea to make him another drink and join the ladies? It was true, Rucker conceded, that there was a lot of drinking that evening. He admitted that – after getting Young away from the ladies, the rector sat in a smoking-room with several men for two hours more, with additional drinks being served. If Rucker was such a dear friend of Young's, why didn't he see the man home, or have his butler do it? "I should not be inclined to send my butler with a drunken clergyman," Rucker snapped. Rawlinson suggested that Rucker had anointed himself leader in a plot to remove Mr. Young. The witness said he was only one of several concerned people in Chipstead. Had not Mr. Young raised issues before the District Council regarding housing for the labourers at Reeves Rest? It was such a minor issue, so long ago, that Rucker allowed he did not recollect the matter.

Bale, the groom at Sothern Farm, recalled the rector's midnight visit to complain about the locked gate. He lent Young a light but watched him walk right into a pond.

> Q: (Rawlinson) When Mr. Young found himself in the pond, what did he do?

A: He turned around and walked back out.
Dibdin (from the bench): Exactly what any reasonable man would have done! [Much laughter]

Mr. Garle was called to describe his being aghast at Young's dinner talk about the rectory housemaid. The rector had offered Garle her services as a naked artist's model, but warned him, "Hands Off!" The rector had quickly downed three glasses of port, "I counted." The witness did not remember Mrs. Young telling him that her husband had been made very ill that day by a vaccination.

The parade of Chipstead witnesses continued. Miss Lillian Phill, village schoolmistress, suspected the rector had been drinking on several occasions. In drink, he would frighten the children with his loud voice, exhorting the young scholars to "Buck up!" Goronwy Prothero, the organist and choirmaster, repeatedly clashed with the rector. On one occasion, the rector halted choir practice, complaining, "Prothero, hold 'Heaven' any longer and we'll never get there." The organist thought the rector had been drinking the day he grabbed him by the coat and threatened him, "If you oppose me, you'll find me a warm one." Pinnock, a waiter at Laker's Hotel in Redhill, had often served the rector who used to come in after his meetings in Reigate. One day, after a couple of drinks in half-an-hour, Young had to be helped into his trap. Pinnock later heard that there had been an accident. The local constable, PC West, who had been at the scene of such spills, thought the rector had been drinking.

But West admitted he nevertheless signed the village testimonial passed around by the rector's remaining friends.

> We, the undersigned parishioners of Chipstead, hearing of your rumored departure, wish to express the regret which you leaving us will occasion, and to assure you of our personal regard and esteem.

The constable said he had signed it just to be nice.

The most damaging and poignant testimony came from the Norrises of Longshaw. Edith Norris and Mrs. Young were close friends. The rector had done a wedding one day in 1899 and afterwards, everyone went back to Longshaw. Arthur Norris testified that Young was in heartiest, back-slapping mood that day, at one point shouting, "Am I to have no blooming drink?" The rector finally had some claret, spilled one glass and soon began carrying on outrageously; eventually he was found in the kitchen, drinking with the cook. Dibdin barked at the chuckling gallery, "None of this is funny." Norris testified that Young was "absolutely" drunk. Norris wanted to throw the man out of his house but his wife stopped him. Mrs. Norris followed, testifying to what had been a very upsetting day. The rector drank a lot of claret and became utterly foolish. Dibdin intervened to ask, "What was your conclusion?" She answered, "Oh, he was undoubtedly drunk." She recalled walking with the rector in the garden at Longshaw, pleading with him to stop drinking. Mrs. Young cried for several hours. Questioned by Rawlinson, Mrs.

Norris admitted that despite this "upsetting" day, she still allowed her daughter to visit and occasionally stay at the rectory with the Youngs.

>A: Yes, I am afraid I was very foolish. I rely on Mrs. Young being there. I rather keep away from the rectory myself.
>
>Rawlinson: Oh, I see, it is alright for your daughter but you are very cautious about yourself.

The cricket incident provided lighter moments. The Rev. Mr. Young's activity with the Chipstead club seems to have waned in the late 1890's but in 1900 he was once again a regular player. On 30 June, he had played for the Chipstead Married XI, losers to the Chipstead Singles. He was no longer captain; Frank Goad, of The Lodge, Chipstead, a hides and tallow merchant, had replaced him. On 28 July, Goad assigned the rector to be wicketkeeper in an away match with Outwood. After the morning innings, there was lunch, with food and drink from the Prince of Wales inn. Goad testified that, after "lunch," Young became quite noisy. He was jumping about, shouting and gesticulating to the other Chipstead players, until, finding himself in front of the wickets, he fell over them twice. After the match, the rector was found sprawled on the grass. Rawlinson reminded Goad that the rector had performed well as a batsman; he'd "been in" for more than a half hour, making the top score for Chipstead. "I dare say," Goad replied coolly. The captain also acknowledged that it had been an exciting day of sport, much shouting was heard and many players were left exhausted.

George Brickett, who regularly played for Reigate Priory, had been on the Chipstead side that day. He testified to Young's over-excited shouting and jumping about. Brickett thought that the rector's conduct as wicket-keeper was unaccountable for a man of his experience. No one would ever get out in front of the wickets.
   Q: Even in Chipstead cricket? (laughter)
   A: Even in Chipstead cricket.
   Q: In Reigate Priory cricket?
   A: No, Reigate Priory is a class above Chipstead cricket.

As for the Alsatian Club, Inspector Edward Drew, of the "C" Division in Vine Street, knew it well, having raided the place on at least two occasions. "Tricky" Drew, as he was known to friend and foe, informed the court that the club had finally been closed. In 1899, when the Rev. Young was found there, it was a "well known resort for ladies of the town."

Wentworth Cattley, now the owner of Shabden Park upon the death of his uncle, testified that he, his brother Guy and Henry Butler had arrived at the Alsatian at 1:30. *In the morning.* He was surprised to see the Rev. Young in the upstairs dancing-room seated with a lady in a white evening dress upon his knee. "Did he seem to resent it," Gill asked. "No, I don't think so," Cattley laughed. The witness said that anyone of ordinary intelligence would quickly know what kind of ladies were in the club. Enough about the ladies, Rawlinson wanted Cattley's thoughts about the gentlemen who would patronise such a place? Are we to assume they were all there for an immoral purpose? If he presumed there was something wrong with Mr. Young being there, what of his attendance? Why had Mr. Cattley gone there that night? He had only gone to look, "as one would do in Paris," he said. Had not Mr. Young told him he was there to chaperone a young man? Perhaps. Cattley admitted they spoke for ten minutes; but he never protested the clergyman's presence nor suggested that he leave. Nor was Mr. Cattley's opinion of the rector so shaken that he made any objection to Rev. Young later doing the burial service for his uncle.

As Mr. Cattley stepped down, having given his evidence that he had only been at the club "to look," would the assessors have been interested to know that this young single gentleman was actually secretly married but living apart from his wife, while paying her regular sums for her silence? Would his credibility as far as impugning the character of the Rev. Young have been lessened? Quite likely. Cattley was not divorced until 1909.[21]

Guy Ewing followed his brother and had a much rougher time of it. Rawlinson began by asking if he was married. Ewing stated that he and his wife resided in Knightsbridge where he ran a surveying business but he came down to Chipstead very often. Guy and the rector had not gotten along. The witness admitted that he enjoyed "chaffing" the clergyman. "I am afraid I did not hold him in great respect." At the Alsatian, Ewing admitted, "I ragged him, if you know the expression." He freely admitted his actions that night:

>Ewing: I pulled him out of the chair and spanked him.
>Rawlinson: You seriously say that? A married man, shocked to see the parson there, and you did that?
>Ewing: I certainly did. It was a mark of my sense of his unbecoming presence in being there.
>Dibdin: Why did you have no respect for Mr. Young?
>Ewing: Because of his drinking.

Here, one of the assessors, Sir Charles Fox interjected, censuring Ewing's testimony. "It is now far too common this mocking of clergymen," said the baronet. The prosecutor, Mr. Gill agreed, "It is lamentable, one of the most successful plays we have has a clergyman as the chief butt." Guy Ewing stood down but he had not been Mr. Gill's best witness.

Henry Butler was the third member of the Chipstead set that evening. Little attention was paid to the young wine dealer but he may have played the largest role in the Alsatian fiasco. Butler testified that he had also supped that night at the Continental on Lower Regent Street. He looked across the room to see Mr. Young at a crowded table, with both men and women. The rector waved him over to explain that he was chaperoning some lads from Cambridge who were in London for the night. Butler recalled thinking that supper at the Continental was an odd choice for a chaperone because there were "nothing but demi-mondaines" about the place. It is entirely possible that Butler, having seen the rector and his group depart, could have learned they were all "off to the Alsatian." Knowing that the Ewing brothers were also up in town, he might then have searched them out with an idea of following "the old boy" for a bit of fun. It is supposition upon supposition but it does undermine, a bit, the great coincidence of their being at the Alsatian that morning.

On the third day of the Consistory Court, it was time for Rawlinson to begin the case for the defense. He was prepared to present evidence that would directly conflict with every charge that had been made against Mr. Young. His client had worked extremely hard in his years in Chipstead; the congregation had grown, the church had been restored. The work was constant and tiring. Mr. Young was earnest, anxious and - yes - excitable. "If there was a fault to be found with him,' Rawlinson concluded, 'it was his desire to be all things to all men." The assessors would be hearing from both Mr. and Mrs. Young – at last given their chance to frustrate those who would destroy their home and ruin him professionally.

Clara Lambert had worked for ten years at the rectory. On the night Mr. Young returned home from the infamous Rucker party, he was not drunk at all, she testified. He was quite hungry, complaining that he had arrived too late to eat at Reeves Rest. So, she warmed him a pork pie. She saw nothing to indicate, from his trousers or shoes, that he had recently been standing in any water. Morgan, the rector's valet, backed her up. He cleaned the man's shoes daily and there was no mud on them that morning (now almost four years past.) Gill, in his cross-examinations, chose to ignore their testimony, asking the maid and valet instead about the rector's drinking habits, and whether they ever had to help him upstairs to bed. Amy Mings, the kitchen maid of the "fine form," was, of course, a witness of some interest. The "pre-possessing" young lady flatly denied Mr. Garle's testimony. At no time in her presence had the rector said anything about her being an artist's model. She swore that the rector had been so "seedy" that night that Mrs. Young made her apologies to Mr. Garle and the guest left rather early. Young's physician, Dr. John Ogle of Reigate, told the court that he had given the rector a vaccination earlier on the day of the Garle dinner and "he had not taken it well." Ogle said he had not observed any signs that the rector, as his longtime patient, had any problem with alcohol.

Similarly, numerous witnesses contradicted the idea that the Rev. Young had been drunk on the cricket ground in 1900. Francis Peek, the landowner at Outwood, had been deposed and swore he saw nothing objectionable in Young's behavior. William Durrant, umpire at the match, thought that the rector, for a novice, kept the wickets well. As for Mr. Young being prostrate on the ground afterwards, Durrant said it was rarer not to find the players resting on the grass after such an exciting match. Lastly, William Bennett, the parish overseer, produced the scorebook. Mr. Young had played well that day. Bennett was the publican at the Star Inn in Chipstead. Gill suggested that Bennett was known to provide alcohol for various church events. Was it common to have whisky poured during choir practice? "We please ourselves," the landlord drily answered.

Several brother clergymen were called in succession to give character testimony. The familiar theme was that Mr. Young was a dedicated member of the ministry but excitable, and that may have put off some people. He was quite popular with the elderly and the working folks. The vicar of Walton-on-the-Hill, Rev. H.J. Greenhill, chaired the Reigate Board of Guardians. He served with Young for many years until the latter's recent resignation. He praised the Chipstead rector for his commitment to the work and for enlivening their meetings.[22] Young could be "as exuberant as a schoolboy." Gill asked the witness whether it was true that he had urged Young to stop drinking. Greenhill denied it. He had dined with Young on several occasions. Had Greenhill ever dined at the Hotel Continental?

> A: Yes, for a dinner, as I am chaplain of the Surrey Lawyers Club.
> Gill: But that was a dinner. Supper is a little different.
> A: Yes, I think it is. [Laughter]

Greenhill quickly admitted he had never been to the Alsatian club and knew of it only from the public prints.

Beyond her age, (she was 43) very little can be said about Mary Young. There are no photographs and reporters offered no descriptions of her in court. In Chipstead, she handled the usual responsibilities of a clergyman's wife, e.g. St. Margaret's was beautifully decorated for Easter, "Mrs. Young being assisted by Mrs. Rucker, Mrs. Garle …" or the Christmas jumble sale was a success thanks to "Mrs. Young, Mrs. and Miss Norris …" While her husband was out at council meetings, vestry meetings or visiting the sick, Mrs. Young would manage the rectory. She had placed the newspaper advertisements for a "plain cook," etc. Still, she doesn't seem to have been very much "out" in local society; the unhappy day at Longshaw being a rare occasion.

In criminal or civil actions, a wife could not give evidence for or against her husband, except in domestic cases. Mary Young was permitted to appear in the Consistory Court. The efforts to remove her husband had come as a shock to her. She was quite frustrated as so few people understood how "phenomenally excitable" he was. She called him "mercurial." As for the Rucker's party, the dinner for Mr. Garle, the day at the Norrises, Mary Young steadfastly supported her husband. Of course, the assessors might well conclude "what else could she do?" Mrs. Young admitted she may have cried at the Norrises

36

because the day had been so upsetting, but in no way had she "cried for hours."

Mrs. Young, to be sure, had everyone's sympathy for being placed in such an awful position. Mr. Gill posed only a few perfunctory questions. It was interesting to learn that she was away visiting friends "in the North" on the night of her husband's Alsatian escapade. But he had told her of it immediately, she assured Mr. Gill. The prosecutor would be reserving his powder for the featured target who followed her into the witness box.

The Rev. Charles Gordon Young was sworn. He was a tallish man and well-built. His eyes were deep set, the nose strong and Roman. His hair was dark, and described as "crisp and wavy." It is interesting to note that press observers had recorded that Mr. Young, while presumably sober, appeared disturbed several times by the testimony he was hearing. His natural excitability was, perhaps, on display. He was seen frequently scrawling "agitated notes" for his lawyers.

Young told his counsel (Rawlinson) that, since leaving Chipstead, he and Mrs. Young were now living in Battersea where he was volunteering for the celebrated Canon Erskine Clark. For his work in that poor parish, Clark had been made an honorary chaplain to Queen Victoria. Whilst in Chipstead, Young had never shirked an inquiry into his conduct; rather, he had sought one. But "they" only wanted him out. He remembered the Rucker's evening as ending pleasantly. On his walk home that night, he came to the locked gate on the path and he admitted it upset him. He was rather short with young Bale, "I may well have frightened him." As he left the stables, he walked towards the pond, but, "as 99 men out of 100 would have done," he spun about and went another way home. He did not walk into the water. At the rectory, he arrived ravenously hungry and he ate half a pork pie and the top of a cottage loaf. As far as he knew, he still considered Rucker a friend. They had gone shooting together not long thereafter, without incident. Young's evidence was given quite conversationally and produced a good deal of laughter all round.

In likewise fashion, Young, led by Rawlinson, went through all sixteen counts of alleged drunkenness. He wasn't randomly bellowing during the cricket match, he was "coaching and encouraging" his side, especially the younger players. He had once proclaimed that if he couldn't be noisy, he would have to give up cricket. In the pulpit, when he appeared to lose his place and giggle through his readings, Young explained that the scripture that day was from the Acts of the Apostles, (26:14) with the line, "It is hard for you to kick against the goads." With Frank Goad and family in the pews below him, Young said he tried to find - at the last moment - an alternative reading. It had just been a silly moment, with "many titters" in the church. He was not drunk.

Changing subjects, Rawlinson asked if it was true that Young had gone out to Morocco to "dry out."

Absolutely not, the rector replied. He had suffered something very near to a breakdown at that time with the sudden death of a clergyman friend in London.[23] He was unstrung and the only thing for it was a sea voyage. In Morocco, he met Spearing. On their return to London, they dined in a large group at the Continental. He had not a drop of drink. After dinner, although it was very late, he allowed himself to be "over-persuaded" and several of them took hansoms to a club that "I knew absolutely nothing about."

> Q: During the whole time you were there, did you act immorally?
> A: I'm sorry?
> Q: You know what I mean — it has been sworn to that there was a woman sitting on your knee. Is there any truth in that suggestion?
> A: Oh, no, no. None whatever. A woman had come round to the settee where I was sitting and sat close to me. On my knee, no.

When the Chipstead trio arrived, Young told the court, he was actually quite happy to see them, "for the simple reason that I knew nothing of the nature of the club to which I had been taken, and I was thankful to have some respectable friends who would safeguard me under the circumstances." He remained in the Alsatian for no more than forty-five minutes.

The examination concluded with the rector's explanation for his resistance to the repeated calls for him to moderate or eliminate his drinking. He never had a problem with his drinking, he insisted. Yes, he had enjoyed some port, claret, even some whisky, most often in the homes of the same men who were making the charge against him. His exuberance and loudness, the ease at which he showed emotions and his proneness for falls (going back to a concussion of the spine as a boy) were often mistaken for symptoms of drink. He had offered to publicly take the pledge, acknowledging the issue had become a "stumbling block" in the parish but, in reality, Rucker et al just wanted him gone.

The main event was always going to be Mr. Gill's cross-examination of the rector. The prosecutor referred to the various clergymen who had appeared in Mr. Young's support. However, where was Rev. Bott, his first vicar, still there in north London? Young admitted he had not seen him in years. How about Rev. Wodehouse of Merstham, a village two miles away from Chipstead. Young had not asked Mr. Wodehouse. On the voyage to Morocco, did the rector have any alcohol? No, he hadn't. It was only in the mountains, for safety, that he drank some brandy and milk. Gill alleged that on the return voyage, after a few hour's stop in Las Palmas, Young had come back aboard drunk and made a scene because the ship bar was closed? Not true at all. What about in Madeira? Young quipped that he was rather sorry he hadn't brought his diary. Then the questioning turned to the matter of the Alsatian. Young denied having as many as five whiskys that evening. What sort of chaperone takes a young man to such a dubious after-hours club? He thought it was a gambling club but within five minutes, he knew its true nature. Young said, "I told my wife it was a hell on earth." Gill snapped, "Don't bring your wife's name into this." Why hadn't he asked young Spearing to leave? "Undoubtedly, I should have." Three gentlemen from Chipstead had testified that they had seen him with a prostitute upon his knee. Young denied it absolutely.

> A: I was simply sitting looking on. Except when Mr. Ewing pulled me from the chair.
> Q: Do you know that Mr. Ewing said he never treated you with respect?
> A: I am rather afraid it was mutual.

Young admitted that, on previous occasions, he had been to the Trocadero and the Empire Music Hall, London nightclubs not usual venues for clergymen. On one occasion, he had been asked to leave the Empire – but not thrown out - for being too loud, which he blamed on trying to talk over the music.

Getting back to the general charge of drunkenness, Gill reminded the witness that Messrs. Rucker, Garle and Norris had all signed that letter. Why? Young insisted that their memories of events were mistaken; in Mr. Garle's case it was "pure invention." The afternoon at the Norrises followed a morning wedding. Had the rector gone first to the bride's house where he had several glasses of home-made wine? Young said it was one of "the penalties of being a country parson, you have to taste everything." He may have had a single glass, but certainly no cherry brandy. At the Norris home, he always visited the kitchen as he knew the cook very well. He may well have said something about having some "blooming drink" as the language in the Norris home was rather free and easy. "Blooming" was considered a mild curse at the time.[24]

> Q: Did you not feel as a clergyman the need to set an example?
> A: No, I am afraid I followed one.

Young insisted that he preferred to drink lemon smash, sometimes ginger beer. If necessary, when upset or anxious before services, he might have an egg and whisky concoction. It was a remedy he'd learned to rely on while at the Marylebone infirmary, as "the deathbeds were too much for me." When out socially, he drank what was offered. He repeated his willingness to take the pledge. Gill had nothing more.

Rawlinson wanted to make clear that Mr. Young did not mean to say that he needed to take the pledge. Young agreed. He had only offered owing to the "mistaken impressions" that had been formed in Chipstead. He was certain that he could stop drinking at will. He easily quit smoking every Lent and had the diaries to prove it. Mr. Young had been in the witness box for four hours. His demeanour was described as lively throughout but he never lost control and seemed to have acquitted himself rather well under Gill's questioning.

On the second of November, another Saturday session, the day was reserved for the speeches by counsel. Chipstead society had returned to hold down whatever seats they could find in the gallery. This was no ordinary jury to impress or cajole. The five assessors were a trio of veteran clergymen and two prominent laymen. Lewis Dibdin, the Chancellor, was an "impeccable" scholar. Still, they had just heard more than three days of dramatically conflicting evidence. While some of the events in question could have innocently been misinterpreted by one side or the other, there also had to be some perjury going on.

Procedurally, the defense was to go first and Rawlinson spent nearly three hours on his feet, frequently questioned by the assessors. The promoters of the action had accused Rev. Young of being a habitual drunkard, a man with a flask at the ready. That was simply untrue as several professional gentlemen, clergyman and physicians had sworn. The chancellor broke in to say that he agreed, the charge of habitual drinking had failed, in his opinion. But that did not answer the sixteen stipulated incidents of drunkenness. Again, Rawlinson returned to the theme that the rector was a hot-headed, impetuous man whose manner was such as to let some conclude, mistakenly, whether it be on a cricket ground or a drawing room that he was in drink. Mr. Norris' testimony, for instance, was entirely uncorroborated. If Mr. Young was carrying on with the cook, why was she not called? Why did Norris then allow his daughter to spend two months at the rectory? Another missing witness was young Cecil Spearing. Rawlinson believed the details of the Moroccan voyage and that "night out" in London could only have come from Cecil Spearing – a young gentleman who demonstrated a strange way of showing his appreciation for Mr. Young's sickbed attentions. Yet Spearing was not man enough to face an English jury? Why not? Rawlinson granted that it was a mistake for any clergyman to have entered such a place as the Alsatian. But then explain why three church-goers from Chipstead were also in that "noisome place?" Rawlinson said Mr. Young had gone there, in his way of being all things to all men and to see every side of what was sometimes referred to as "the life." He was wrong to have been there but he had committed no ecclesiastical offense. The chancellor interjected, "Even if he was found with a prostitute upon his knee?" Rawlinson reminded the court that Mr. Young had sworn that *did not* happen, but even if it had, Rawlinson argued there was no offense in it, as he had not invited it. Mr. Young had the misfortune to have fallen out with the "moneyed classes" in his village and he urged the panel to view their evidence with "great suspicion." Mrs. Young, a woman whose integrity had never been challenged, had sworn that she had never seen her husband drunk. For several hours, the Rev. Mr. Young had sat before them, withstanding Mr. Gill's rigorous examination. Hot-headed, emotional, Rawlinson conceded his client may well have been. But deceitful, never.

A seemingly confident Mr. Gill took much less time to sum up the case for the promoters. This unpleasant task had been begun for no other reason than because it was in the best interest of the parish of St. Margaret's, Chipstead. There was no animus of class against the rector; witnesses came from all walks of life to London to describe his conduct. In the face of so much evidence, Gill suggested that the defendant had no choice but to put a "bold face" before the public, and he congratulated him on the effort. While questioning Mr. Young, Gill found himself restrained from comment as he heard the rector flatly deny ever being drunk. The prosecutor held back, having no wish to be thought "unkind." Lastly, he certainly disagreed with his learned friend on the question of Mr. Young's presence and behavior at the Alsatian Club. Do not compare the attendance of the three young men with that of a man representing the Church of England. It seemed clear that the defendant had gone there to "make a night of it," and his conduct at that club was plainly "riotous and immoral" as defined by the Clergy Discipline Act. It was impossible that Mr. Young could remain any longer in Chipstead.

The assessors adjourned with Chancellor Dibdin to deliberate. A verdict had to be either the unanimous opinion of the assessors – even if it contradicted the chancellor's finding – or, the opinion of the chancellor and a majority of the assessors. None of that mattered because, within thirty minutes, the chancellor returned to announce that their verdict was unanimous.

Firstly, they found the Rev. Charles Gordon Young not guilty of habitual drunkenness. However, they found him guilty of being drunk on "divers occasions," namely five of the original sixteen incidents, including Mr. Rucker's dinner party and the cricket match in Outwood. As for the Alsatian club, Dibdin agreed that the Rev. Young "had been 'making a night of it.'"

> He had willingly entered a place where no licensing laws – nor any other laws – were observed. There were obviously immoral people present. He went there at 12:30 at night, at the end of an evening spent at various places of entertainment, and then, after realising the character of the place, stayed there for three quarters of an hour, talking and joking with a woman, and behaving himself in the manner described.

By these actions, the Rev. Young had violated the 75th and 109th canons of clerical conduct[25] – the latter proscribes "adultery, whoredom, incest or drunkenness." Even though no specific act of indecency was proven against him, he was guilty of immoral conduct unworthy of a clergyman. The findings would be given to the Bishop of Rochester for his decision and action.

The verdict had come late in the day but there were many partisans remaining, representing either side in the Chipstead dispute. As the chancellor's reading continued and the decision made clear, it was certainly not an occasion for cheering from the promoter's ranks. Dibdin would scarcely have permitted any such outburst. It was all done with rather brutal formality and the assessors retired. If there was a time for tears for Mrs. Young, it had arrived. Her husband knew that the Bishop could do only one thing, pronounce a sentence of deprivation. The secular expression was a harsh one – the rector was to be "unfrocked." Though the Bishop's edict would only apply to the diocese of Rochester, it almost certainly meant an end to Young's career in the Church of England. The story had been reported – in great detail – in newspapers up and down the island, as editors well knew that "there is more interest for the ordinary reader in the peccadilloes of a minister than in those of an ordinary citizen."

Mr. and Mrs. Young thanked their beaten counsel and his associates and went out into the "grey dusk of a late November afternoon." They were followed by what remained of their now forlorn cadre of friends. After some hurried handshakes, the Youngs entered a hansom cab which, rather ominously, had their portmanteau tied to the roof. It was reported that the Youngs were off to the railway station and planned to leave London immediately.

With mocking headlines about the vivacious rector and news of "Parson Young's Night Out," the public had rather expected the verdict and quickly moved on. But in Chipstead and in the larger world of that part of Surrey, there was a sense felt by many that the rector had been ill-treated. The first blast came in a published letter signed by more than a dozen members of the Reigate Rural District Council, including the chairman and five clergymen. They received the news of the Consistory Court's findings with extreme regret. "Mr. Young was favourably regarded and loved by the vast majority of the residents in the council's thirteen parishes." Unnamed Chipstead residents were accused of "hatching" a plot to bring down the rector. No names were necessary. To entertain a gentleman in one's home, serve him alcohol and then tell the whole world about his behaviour, "violates every canon of British hospitality." The strongly worded letter drew a published reply from Charles Sweet expressing his "pain and surprise" at the insinuation that the charges were in anyway trumped up.

The county paper - the *Surrey Mirror* - did not quarrel with the findings but regretted the loss of a clergyman of unquestionable gifts, which had caused "deep regret among all who have the interests of religion at heart." But the leader-writer also found "painful" the manner in which the case had been gotten up in certain corners of Chipstead society. It was, at the least, "very disagreeable." A separate testimonial signed by 220 residents of Chipstead was hand-delivered to the Bishop's palace. It mattered not. As recounted in the opening of this account, the chancellor's verdict was read and the Bishop's sentence pronounced on 19 November 1901. A few days later, the local press announced that "the Rev. C. Gordon Young wishes to thank his many correspondents for their expressions of sympathy, and hopes shortly to be able to reply individually to all."

It was very soon Christmas in Chipstead and the curate-in-charge, the Rev. Mr. Tozer, had the assistance of the Norris ladies and others in the decoration of St. Margaret's which was suitably praised. Tozer, despite his youth, seems to have done quite well during what was acknowledged to be "a period of great difficulty." Thus, on Easter Sunday, 1902, there was some disappointment when the curate announced that he was to be replaced. He had enjoyed his year in the parish and hoped he had been part of the healing. In his sermon, he reminded his listeners that "Easter summons us to the newness of life. Let all bitter thoughts and feelings now sink and be buried in the grave of the past." Well said, indeed.

As mentioned previously, the patron of Chipstead was the Baron Hylton. The old baron, who'd been happy enough to hand the living to Mr. Young, had passed away. His successor raised the bar, and the Rev. James Hervey was to succeed to Chipstead rectory. Hervey was a nephew of the Marquis of Bristol and the fourth son of the Bishop of Bath & Wells. The Chipstead gentry must have been well chuffed to know their new rector was of the peerage and the purple. Hervey was in Chipstead for many years and built up the most positive reputation but he was never the man for cricket that Mr. Young had been.

The Chipstead banishment seems to have put paid to Mr. Young's clerical career. The last official trace of the erstwhile rector was in the census for 1901 where he and his wife were found living in Battersea. It is a commonplace to end such stories with a comment that so-and-so is "living quietly" but in the Rev. Young's case that seems most unlikely.

Last Word: In 1907, there was a report that not Reverend but *Mister* C. Gordon Young had been appointed honorary secretary of the Income Tax Reduction League. Nothing seems to have come of that. In 1908, the editor of the *Surrey Mirror*, published in Reigate, wrote that he happened to run into the former clergyman one spring afternoon:

> Mr. Young's appearance is somewhat altered since he resided in this district, as he now grows a full beard and moustache. As a result, he went unrecognised by many with whom he was at one time well acquainted, in a stroll through the Redhill streets[26].

The brief account does not reveal whether Mr. Young took the time to look up any of his former parishioners in Chipstead.

2. A CASE OF HEARTLESS VILLAINY

"What are we to think of the young women who yielded to the advances of a scrofulous parson with one leg?"[27]

Batcombe Church (2016). The front cross marks the Brown family graves.

It was a small group of mourners that gathered on a wintry day in the "pretty and secluded" Somerset village of Batcombe. They stood beside a freshly dug grave in the churchyard of St. Mary the Virgin. Looming above them was "one of the last of Somerset's mighty towers,"[28] from which the bells had tolled solemnly. The rector's wife of more than forty years had died rather suddenly on 3 March 1877. She had been ill for some time; her condition had required long stays in the sea air at Weston-super-Mare. Showing some improvement, she'd returned to the rectory. The parish curate had dined with her only the day before her death. She seemed "perfectly well" and he recalled a pleasant meal and conversation with Mrs. Brown. But, during the night, very quickly she was gone. There was an inquest. She had suffered an apoplectic fit and, mercifully, her struggle was over.

The newly widowed Rev. John Brown was 72-years old and in poor health himself. The aforementioned curate, the Irish-born Samuel Roden Henderson, officiated at the funeral. The deceased was very well-known and respected and people came from many of the nearby villages: Westcombe, Upton-cum-Noble, Evercreech and, of course, Batcombe. The grieving rector was supported by his two daughters. Susanna[29], his youngest, was unmarried, nearly 40, and, as with so many of her ilk, she had been her aging father's housekeeper. Her older sister, Charlotte, had come down from London without her husband. She'd been married for more than twenty years to the Rev. Richard Marsh Watson, but owing to his own serious health issues, he remained in the city.

The Browns had been living in genteel poverty in Batcombe for some time. The rectory on Gold Hill was a splendid old pile but in need of repair. The previous year, the rector, for reasons of finance and failing health, had tried to sell his advowson, or his right to the church and rectory. Despite the beautiful church in a "delightfully situated" village, the income from the scattered rural parish was not one that generated a satisfactory offer and the sale was withdrawn. After Mrs. Brown's death, a decision had to be made. No longer able to handle the liturgical and temporal duties required, the Rev. Brown decided to give up the rectory, putting it up for let. The rector and his daughter Susanna moved to Bath. Mr. Henderson, the curate, handled the duties at St. Mary's and resided in rooms locally.

Susanna, Charlotte and their surviving brother, had received some small annuities from their mother's estate. A little over two months after Mrs. Brown's death, Susanna received a letter addressed to her at 1, Queen's Square, Bath. The full contents of the letter were never publicly revealed as certain unrelated family matters were discussed in it. In the section of the letter that generated this extraordinary scandal, the writer demanded from Miss Susanna Brown the sum of £200 or "the whole story will be placed before your father." Denials would be unavailing, so the letter-writer insisted. Documentary evidence had been preserved and several witnesses were still living and willing to talk.

The letter did not shock Miss Brown. She had received similar threats over the previous decade plus and had paid many times over sums to preserve the writer's silence. But in 1875, she had finally declared herself unable to pay anymore. There was no use asking her for more money. Then, within weeks of her receipt of a small inheritance from her late mother, her tormentor took up his menacing pen once again. But Susanna had determined that there was to be an end to this. Let the world know the worst of her, she would be finished with this campaign of extortion. Let the world know all about her brother-in-law, the Rev. Richard Marsh Watson.

*****

Richard was born in 1826, the middle of three sons, all of whom would become clergymen. Their father was a solicitor in Canterbury. The Watson family was an influential one, residing for a time within the Cathedral close. The boys all attended the King's School; the eldest, James, and the youngest, Henry, served as "Captains" of the school during their respective years. The archivist[30] at King's reports that there are "gaps" in the records of Richard's school years. After King's, he does not appear to have attended university, while both brothers took degrees at Cambridge (Corpus Christi). Richard, unfortunately, was a sickly youth, afflicted with the dreaded "King's Evil," scrofula.

Scrofula[31] comes from the Latin word for a sow, a female pig. Typically, the disease affected the lymph glands of the throat and neck; they became swollen and distorted until they eventually burst emitting "cheesy" substances. In the middle-ages, it was thought the only cure was to be touched by the King. Edward the Confessor was the first English monarch to claim that healing power. Victorian physicians had closely linked scrofula with tuberculosis and there was yet no cure. Treatments were surgical and involved "scooping" and "cupping." The resulting "unsightly scars" contributed to the general public impression of the scrofulous person as "repulsive." But scrofula could spread elsewhere in the body and "diseases of bone form one of the most frequent and most serious of the manifestations of scrofula." Children and adolescents with scrofula were instructed to avoid rough play and games as their limbs were much more susceptible to fracture. When he was 21, Richard had his right leg amputated at the knee. He was one of the last patients of the legendary surgeon Dr. Robert Liston, known as "the fastest knife in the West End."[32]

On the bright side, it must be supposed, was the widely held belief that scrofulous children were "unduly intelligent and precocious." Sir Frederick Treves debunked the theory by suggesting that "the scrofulous child is the delicate one of the family. Perhaps it is petted, has more notice taken of it, and is offered every facility for the development of the points that make up the 'precocious infant.'"[33] The great Treves aside, Richard was clearly an intelligent young man, just not strong enough for the rigours and occasional brutality of a Victorian education. He was extremely well-read and an organist of some skill. In his early 20's, Richard went to live with his uncle, the Rev. George Henry Marsh at his rectory in Great Snoring in Norfolk. Marsh was the son of the late Bishop of Peterborough. Richard was a popular fellow in the village, he paid for the new organ in the church, and assisted in the fetes and treats for the local children, all of whom were fascinated by "Mr. Watson's artificial leg."

Since Dr. Liston's swift procedure, Richard had endured seven years of "the usual course of torture which arises from the use of badly constructed artificial limbs." Enter Frederick Gray of Bond Street whose new technologies had proven so beneficial that Richard had allowed his name to feature in a new advertisement:

> Now, in bearing this grateful testimony to your abilities and skill, a query arises in my mind, "Must these great blessings be confined to the rich alone?" Cannot some plan be devised by which the poor might partake of these inestimable benefits, and you, at the same time, have your rightful interests protected? So deeply do I

sympathize with my poorer fellow-sufferers that I declare myself ready to come forward at once, and devote my whole time and energies in endeavouring to found a society that shall have for its object the providing of artificial legs and arms of your make, to those who from their needy circumstances are unable to procure them. I will commence the subscription list with a donation of Two Hundred Guineas, and be further prepared with pecuniary support, should the public (as I will not believe) be slow in seconding me. I remain, yours very faithfully, R. Marsh Watson.[34]

Meantime, in 1851, the eldest son of the rector of Batcombe, George Francis Brown, home from his studies at Cambridge, was out shooting. Whilst trying to get through a fence, his gun discharged; the shot struck him fully in one leg. The wound was not thought serious at first but it never healed and, eventually, an amputation was required. Mere coincidence, perhaps. But it is entirely possible that the shared need for an artificial appliance to replace a lost limb brought Richard Marsh Watson and the Brown family of Batcombe together.

Batcombe was and is ever the perfect setting for a wedding. "The view of the church rising above its village is incomparable."[35] On Tuesday, 11 September 1855, the sun shone with "unwonted brilliancy" across the harvest-ready fields of Somerset, as Richard Marsh Watson, "gentleman,"

59

was married to Charlotte Augusta Brown, "spinster." The groom was 29, the bride 20. Knowing of Richard's condition, as the Browns undeniably did, brought a shade over this otherwise happy occasion. A leading expert had only recently declared: "No private individual, who has any rational regard for his future progeny or his own happiness, should marry a scrofulous person."[36]

Richard's health had been somewhat stronger and, bolstered by his new leg, he had begun studies at Lincoln's Inn with an eye on a career at the bar. But he abandoned the law and instead entered the Chichester Theological College. Founded as recently as 1839, at the height of the Tractarian controversy, the college was known for its "High Church bias." By the mid-1850's, however, enrollment was in decline. As few as five students were being admitted each year. Richard proceeded well in his studies and continued to attract favourable notice. In 1857, he gave a lecture on the Isle of Wight on "The Life of John Bunyan" which was very well-received. The local newspaper noted that young Mr. Watson was preparing for his ordination and he will be "an acquisition to any parish which may be fortunate enough to secure his pastoral superintendence."[37] The newspaper also reported that "Mr. and Mrs. Marsh Watson" were staying in Ryde, accompanied by "Miss Brown."

In Salisbury Cathedral on 30 May 1858, Richard Marsh Watson was ordained a clerk in holy orders.

His first assignment was as curate in the Dorset village of Langton Maltravers. But he - and Charlotte, of course - remained not very long among the quarrymen and their families near the Channel. By 1859, he was in Bristol, still a curate, but at the splendid Gothic church of St. Mary Redcliffe, once described as "the most famous parish church in England." Alas, health problems intervened again and on 11 August 1860, it was reported that the "much beloved and assiduous" Rev. Mr. Watson would be forced to relinquish his duties as senior curate. Perhaps the duties in such a populous parish were simply too much for him because Charlotte and he are next to be found in the small village of North Kelsey in Lincolnshire. Briefly. The appointment there was a temporary one and the Watsons soon moved to London where, again for only a short time, he served as a curate at the church of St. Andrew's Undershaft in the City. For whatever reason, most likely his delicate health, Richard's last official church employment was at St. Andrew's in London. He continued to appear in the various clergy lists and directories; he reported himself as a "clergyman" in the census and he did an occasional wedding.

If preaching and parish work were too much for him, Richard could make a church-related living with his knowledge and his writing. In 1862, he published a collection entitled *Original Plain Practical Sermons.* The book contained several sermons commenting on various readings from scripture. If there was one common complaint among the overworked clergymen of the Church of

England, it was the drudgery of writing a weekly sermon. Thus was the market created for "sermon-mongers." Exclusivity was important; in *The English Churchman*, the advertisement for Watson's sermons promised

> The circulation of this Lithographic Periodical is exclusively confined to the Clergy. Terms to subscribers: A Quarter's Sermons viz., Thirteen Sermons 13s 6d. Other sermons charged for according to the subject. No second copy of a sermon will be sent within reach of another Subscriber.

> St. Matthew XVIII. 12.13. "How think ye? If a man have an hundred Sheep, & one of them be gone astray, doth he not leave the ninety & nine, & goeth into the mountains, & seeketh that which is gone astray? And if so be that he find it, verily I say unto you, he rejoiceth more of that sheep, than of the ninety & nine which went not astray".
>
> There are many passages of Scripture which tell us of God's love to perishing sinners, & His desire that not one of them should perish, but that all might come to Him & be saved. But there are few, that bring that love & desire, more forcibly before us, than this text. — Here Christ speaks, of an every day occurrence,

A "lithographed" detail from Watson's *Original Plain Practical Sermons*.

Note the reference to the "lithographed" sermon format. The sermons were not set in type but rather written out in a very formal and plain penmanship. This was a clever ploy in the trade, as it deceived the sharp-eyed parishioner:

> What they took to be MS. sermons, were in reality sermons in lithograph, imitating hand-writing, to deceive such observers into the belief that the preacher composed his sermons, and that the writing was very plain, lest any halting of the reverend reader should betray his want of acquaintance with the manuscript.[38]

Another money-making scheme of Watson's was the idea to start a school in Blackheath, near London. The exact particulars of this venture do not survive but many unbeneficed clergymen found employment in education. The new school was to be a family venture with Charlotte being one of the instructors and, in 1864, Susanna Brown came to stay with the Watsons, perhaps intending to remain as a teacher or governess of some sort. Early in 1864, Charlotte was absent for some length of time. During his wife's absence, Richard seduced his sister-in-law. We are asked to believe that Susanna never told her sister of her husband's betrayal and, moreover, she was also able to hide her resulting pregnancy and deliver the child unbeknownst to her older sibling.

Susanna's child, a son, was born three days after Christmas 1864, at 20 Craven Terrace in Bayswater. That address seems to have been a "lying-in home" for women, of at least some means, seeking to be privately confined up to their delivery. The infant was christened at St. Augustine's Church in Watling Street on 5 February 1865. Three days later, the birth of "Herbert Edward Stanley Brown" was registered in Paddington. On the birth certificate, in the box for the mother's name, "Susanna Brown" was entered. The box for the father's name was left blank. This was standard for an illegitimate birth. However, at this time (and until 1875), the registration rules allowed a woman to name the man she believed to be the father of the child.[39] Susanna chose not to reveal her seducer's name, keeping - perhaps for the first but certainly not for the last time - Richard Marsh Watson's secret. If she expected anything from that gesture, she was to be bitterly disappointed. "From that time to this,' Susanna declared in 1877, '[he] has more or less threatened me."

Whatever happened to little baby Herbert? The child cannot be traced. The best case would have been adoption, perhaps a home could be found for the child on the continent. What chance did Herbert have if anyone knew his father was scrofulous? Scrofula was not a disease that manifested itself in infancy, typically the signs began at around the age of three. Who could predict the boy's future? Medical science remained divided upon the question of the direct inheritance of scrofula. Some believed the likelihood was greater with a scrofulous mother. Regardless, as suggested earlier, doctors held a "decidedly unfavourable" opinion on the advisability of marriage with a scrofulous individual. However, this was a connexion outside marriage, which will happen:

> Human nature and selfishness are inseparable, and if man will seek gratification even at the risk of his own health or life, it cannot be expected that he will be deterred from the pursuit of it by any considerations having reference to beings yet unborn.[40]

The worst case possibilities for Herbert, as usual, were more numerous. If the infant was abandoned, the authorities would have pressed Susanna to "summons" the father to support the child. There is no record of that. The 1860's were also a time when the grimmest "baby-farmers" thrived in Britain. In conclusion, given that the child was not mentioned in any of the legal proceedings – other than the fact of his birth and registration – Herbert was likely dead by the time his father's disgrace was broadcast across England.

Richard and Charlotte Watson, perhaps advisedly, had no children of their own. After the Blackheath venture foundered, they moved on, never staying in any one place for very long. They lived in Brighton for a while; in the 1871 census, they were living in Penge; in 1877, they were living in Notting Hill. However much money Watson could have extorted from a Somerset spinster, it would hardly be enough to support him and his wife. Again, he had found work in church-related employment, if of the dubious variety. He was an "ecclesiastical agent" employed by Messrs. Seymour & Co. of 3, Mill

Street, Conduit Street, W. Mayfair. The back pages of all the various church magazines were filled with advertisements from agencies such as the Messrs. Seymour. Some clergymen were looking to sell out, others to buy: "Presentation wanted to purchase by the friends of a clergyman. Must be a desirable benefice." Such trading in the selling of "livings" was always on the edge of propriety, occasionally rising to the level of outright simony and scandal. Parliamentary hearings were held in 1874:

> Q: As a rule, it is rather the black sheep of the profession that gather round the doors of these clerical agents than otherwise?
> A: Yes, I think they are not the best sort.[41]

The letter to Susanna Brown with the threat to place the "whole matter in front of her father" had been posted from the offices of Messrs. Seymour.

Susanna, as described, was newly-committed to resist any more threats. She could not consult her father, of course. He had just buried Mrs. Brown and the rector's health was such that he might not survive the news of his treasured daughter's sin and disgrace. Instead, she brought the letter to the Batcombe curate, Mr. Henderson. He would play the role of her knight errant.

On 16 May 1877, Rev. Henderson arrived from Bath at the Great Western Railway's Paddington terminus and went immediately to Mill Street. More alley than street, the lane ran behind St. George's Hanover Square, connecting with Savile Row. It was home to several lower-end tailors and small offices. The curate entered Number 3. A clerk greeted him and insisted that he was the only person present but instructions had been left by his employer that no discussion of the matter referred to in that letter would be held with anyone but the recipient, Miss Susanna Brown. Henderson retreated but assured the clerk that the friends of Miss Brown were determined that this persecution must cease.

On the following day, at about two p.m., Henderson returned accompanied by two detectives from the "C" Division. Detective William Cave did the talking. Once again the clerk at the ecclesiastical agency was grieved to report that his employer was not present. There was an inner office, the doorway hidden behind a thick curtain. The detective said he would like to have a look for himself. The clerk tried to physically block the officer and a struggle began but the prompt arrival of young detective Pickles who had been left to watch outside quickly brought order once again. When Cave pulled aside the curtain, he walked in upon a one-legged man attempting to destroy or conceal some papers. Ordered to stop and step away from the desk in front of him, the man identified himself as one of the Messrs. Seymour, ecclesiastical agents. But the Rev. Henderson was present to identify the gentleman as the Rev. Richard Marsh Watson. Cave presented a warrant charging Watson with writing a letter with menaces to a Miss Brown. Watson insisted he wanted no more trouble. "It is all right. What's the best thing to be done?" When told he would have to come along to the police court at Great Marlborough Street, Watson protested that he would need to find counsel. He was prepared "to come up" on any date of the court's choosing. Detective Cave's report concluded: "I said he would have to come and he came away with me."

The veteran magistrate R.M. Newton, hearing Cave's account of the arrest, seemed more outraged that the belligerent clerk had not been put in custody as well. "Twas nothing we couldn't handle," the detective boasted. "That's not the point,' Newton blustered, 'police serving a warrant should not be assaulted." As for the accused in court that afternoon, Watson identified himself as a "clerk in holy orders," the legal term for a clergyman of the Church of England. He was to be charged under Section 44 of the Larceny Act[42] for sending a "letter or writing demanding of any person with menaces, and without any reasonable or probable cause, any property, chattel, money, or valuable security, or other valuable thing." The crime was a felony and upon conviction, the sender faced a sentence of penal servitude for life. This was a crime beyond the scope of a police magistrate's court; Newton ordered Watson to be held without bail in the cells at Clerkenwell. It was ten days before he was formally charged. A lawyer had been found: Henry Kisch insisted his client's health could not endure the cells and he was as deserving of as much consideration as the "prosecutrix," i.e. Miss Brown. The appearance was brief. Newton was rid of Watson's case, transferred to the Central Criminal Court. Bail was again refused and the accused was taken off to Newgate prison in a forbidding police van. At first, the case got rather lost in the lengthy police court reports in the London papers but *Lloyd's*, a weekly journal, headlined their account: "A Villain in Holy Orders," suggesting "the case is likely to excite considerable public interest."

The reason for such interest was plain. The tale that unfolded at the Old Bailey on 28 May was a real-life example of the blackmail and extortion plots that delighted "sensation" novel readers in mid-Victorian England. It illustrated the "essential unknowability" of "the innumerable mysteries behind the facade,"[43] of, for instance, the Batcombe rectory on Gold Hill. Typically, the blackmailer/extortioner would solicit money in exchange for silence, promising not to share the knowledge of something that was either illegal or shameful or both. But Susanna had done nothing "illegal."[44] This was all about her desire to avoid public exposure and shame. In 1877, for Watson to reveal Susanna's fall would have meant her certain disgrace among family and friends and society in general. But he was a co-conspirator in her fall! By revealing all to his father-in-law, Watson would also reveal himself to be an adulterer, likely ruining his own marriage and what - if anything - was left of his very tattered clerical career. Susanna could just have easily extorted money from him. Dozens of clergymen were blackmailed and threatened in such cases. Yet for ten years, Watson held such a powerful sway over this country woman that she purchased her respectability.

At the Old Bailey, Richard Marsh Watson was brought up from his cell below, assisted up the dock stairs to "stand at the bar" before Justice Baron Huddleston. Given the nature of the charge against him, it is unlikely that the one-legged defendant would have been allowed the courtesy of a chair. A press account described him as "tall and gentlemanly looking." He was 51 years old, actually 5-foot-8, with grey hair. Whether they were visible or not in court, Watson bore several scars on his neck and throat (and elsewhere), typical of the "scrofulous."[45] The defendant's brief had been placed in the hands of the legendary figure at the bar, Serjeant William Ballantine.

Susanna Brown was not in court that Wednesday. Her deposition was read out and reported extensively in the press, making clear the exposure she had feared since 1864. She admitted that, in that year, she went to Blackheath to stay with her sister and husband, the defendant. "While staying with them, the prisoner took advantage of me and, as a consequence, I went to Craven-terrace for a short time." She had never revealed her secret to anyone. "From that time to this, the prisoner has more or less threatened me," she swore. The letter of 11 May 1877 was introduced but not read in court. Clearly the letter met the standard of demanding money "with menaces." The Rev. Mr. Henderson followed with the story of his visits to Mill Street. Ballantine pounced upon Henderson's statement that – on his first visit – he had told the clerk that he had come prepared to pay the £200 but only in return for a statement marked "Paid in

70

Full." The serjeant wondered, "Was that Miss Brown's intention all along, to pay again?" Had all this trouble been off Henderson's bat? Henderson insisted that Miss Brown and he had agreed to bring in the police.

After the testimony of the detectives, Ballantine rose to inform the bench that nothing further would be required from the prosecution, as "with his entire concurrence," Mr. Watson had decided to enter a plea of guilty. In exchange for the plea, Ballantine asked that sentencing be delayed until the next sessions so that "certain facts" could be laid before the court which might influence his lordship in passing sentence. It was agreed and Watson was returned to the subterranean warren leading to his Newgate cell.

Four weeks later, when Watson stood again in the dock in the Old Court, he looked down on a new cast of bench and bar. Justice Sir Robert Lush presided. The case for the Crown was left to Digby Seymour, the son of an Irish clergyman, and no relation to the Messrs. Seymour. The guilty plea had been entered; the only issue was sentencing. The crime carried a possible life sentence. Mr. Seymour admitted it was shocking to look upon a man gifted with the advantages of birth and education being charged with such a terrible crime. The defendant, however, had admitted to persecuting Miss Brown for more than a decade until she had no money left. Then, whilst still grieving for her late mother, she received a small inheritance, only to have the prisoner immediately renew his "threats to expose the shame of which he was the author." The prosecution was also ready with additional "certain facts." Seymour presented a document - one of several of its type, he stated – that was found in the papers that the prisoner had been trying to destroy or conceal on the day of his arrest. It was dated 23 September 1876:

> "I, Emily[46], take you, Richard Marsh Watson, from this day forth, to be my wedded husband, and I now swear to live with you as your faithful wedded wife, and shall lawfully marry you as soon as you are free, but shall, in the meantime, live with you as your lawful wedded wife; and I swear this in the name of the Father, Son, and Holy Ghost."

For a clergyman, of whatever status in his church, to blaspheme Our Lord in a contract of such depravity was "an unmitigated atrocity," insisted Seymour. There were other documents like it. The man was incorrigible and deserving of no mercy whatsoever, the prosecutor stated in closing.

Watson's case was now left to Douglas Straight, reputedly one of the "smartest and most attractive men in London." The former attribute would be more germane as Straight would have to wangle for a measure of mercy for the prisoner. Mr. Watson's conduct had been "indefensible," Straight conceded, and it had been his intention to say very little. However, he had been dissuaded from a passive role by "the unusual course that had been taken by his learned friend (Seymour) in pressing the charge with so much severity." He reminded the bench that from the day of his arrest, Mr. Watson had done nothing but co-operate. He had plead guilty at his first opportunity and expressed his sincere regrets to the prosecutrix. Throughout the legal proceedings, "he had instructed his counsel not to put any questions to Miss Brown that would cause her the slightest pain." Nor had he permitted his counsel to raise any matters which "might have been considered some justification" for his demands. This appears to be the only reference to the "certain facts" that Ballentine had previously suggested. There was no explanation given but readers are referred to the sequel below. Despite his remorse and co-operation, Watson, though yet convicted of nothing - had been held in jail - under very cruel conditions which Straight asserted were more barbaric for a man in such delicate health. The life of Richard Marsh Watson had been a most difficult one. The merciless "seeds of scrofula" had prevented him from holding any lasting employment, leading to great "pecuniary pressures." Straight concluded by again stressing Watson's deep repentance and, if not for the man himself, he was deserving of some consideration for the members of the Watson family "several of whom hold high and honourable positions."

Justice Lush was known for an unfailing urbanity; if given a chance, he "never played to the gallery." He took little time before addressing the defendant before him:

> I have paid great attention to this case and all the facts brought before me. I have come to the conclusion this is a case of heartless villainy such as is seldom met with. I believe that you have been carrying on a career of villainy for many years, and it is hardly possible to conceive of anything worse than your conduct in endeavouring to extort money from the prosecutrix by threatening to expose facts of which you are the cause.

The new letters indicated that Watson had been carrying on a system of "getting young women into his power for the purpose of seduction." Lush concluded that the "least sentence" for Richard Marsh Watson was that he be kept in penal servitude for twelve years.

Thus, without any serious quibble, ended the "Extraordinary Trial of a Clergyman." There were suggestions that such painful cases should be heard "in camera." The *Daily Telegraph*, for instance, commented: "The unfortunate lady is relieved, it is true, from the persecution under which she has lain for years; but on the other hand, the whole story of her shame has been made public." As for Watson, no consideration was offered. His sentence was "richly-merited," and let the gates close behind "this thing called a man, a vile scoundrel who goes to his doom without one word of commiseration from any living creature." The publicity drawn to the scandal had also brought forward several clergymen – former purchasers of Watson's "Plain, Practical Sermons," who claimed that, once ensnared, they were forced to continue paying lest Watson reveal to the congregations that the elegant and comforting words of their preacher were not his own[47]. "The Clerical Extortioner" was to serve his sentence at the Woking Invalid Prison; behind an 18-foot wall, the facility built about 1860, housed prisoners with physical and mental disabilities.

Through all this, very little had been heard from Charlotte Watson, whose betrayal by her husband had also been made known to the world. In addition to his seduction of Susanna, Watson had actually prevailed upon another woman (Emily?) to live with him as his wife until he was free to marry her. What was Charlotte's possible fate? On 9 November 1877 – Charlotte filed for a divorce[48] from Richard but the case was not heard until the following February. The grounds for the divorce was her husband's "incestuous adultery w/Susanna Brown, my natural and lawful sister." Incestuous adultery was defined as adultery committed by a husband with "a woman whom, if his wife were dead, he could not lawfully marry, by reason of her being within the prohibited degrees of consanguinity or affinity." The law forbade Richard from ever marrying his deceased wife's sister. Susanna was his wife's sister. Richard could never marry Susanna. Of course, questions would be asked whether it was really possible for Charlotte not to know of the relationship between her sister and husband. Had she known it for any length of time, the issue of condonation would have been raised. Charlotte swore, however, that she had no knowledge of her husband's seduction of Susanna or the birth of their child. Upon her husband's arrest, in his papers, she found the registry of the birth of Herbert Edward Stanley Brown. Susanna testified at the divorce hearing, retelling the story of her disgrace in Blackheath and delivery in Bayswater. Watson did not offer a defence and the decree nisi was granted.

The lives of both Charlotte and Susanna had been ruined by this man. Still, "what are we to think of the young *women* who yielded to the advances of a scrofulous parson with one leg?" The brutal question was posed in a commentary on the trial in the weekly, *The Era*. That question was certainly asked in 1877 but may well have been asked as far back as 1855 when Charlotte and Richard were married in Batcombe. At least then, there was the hope and promise of youth. But by 1865, a decade later, Watson was broken in health and prospects when he seduced his sister-in-law. What was Susanna thinking? By the second half of the nineteenth century, the number of marriageable "spinsters," single women between 20 and 40, outnumbered unmarried men of the same age. 20% of those "bachelors," moreover, it was believed, would never marry.

> There is an enormous and increasing number of single women in the nation, a number quite disproportionate and quite abnormal, a number which, positively and relatively, is indicative of an unwholesome social state, and is both productive and

prognostic of much wretchedness and wrong.[49]

Words like "superfluous" and "redundant" were used to describe the women who found themselves without a husband. Numerous schemes to "emigrate" these extra women to the colonies were launched with varying results. Meantime, the *Era* concluded, "This story is absolutely appalling in its exposition of heartlessness on one side and weakness on the other."[50]

***

To bring our story to a close, a few brief notes.

In the summer of 1878, the Rev. John Brown of Batcombe died in Cheltenham, where he had been living in retirement. What must he have thought of the twice-over scandal affecting his two respectable daughters? His eldest son, the Rev. George Brown, who may be remembered for losing a leg in a shooting accident, died in 1872, leaving a widow and child. In 1878, the widow, Rosalind Brown married Henry Wickham, a much older man, and the head of one of the leading families of Batcombe. The Wickhams went to live in Eastbourne - the newly fashionable resort on the Channel - and Susanna went with them. They lived in one of the numerous boarding houses in which Terrence Rattigan much later chose to set his play, *Separate Tables*. Susanna was, perhaps, one of the first to come to Eastbourne to "escape" some unpleasantness. Charlotte, divorced but still answering to "Mrs. Watson," resided in London.

In 1881, Richard Marsh Watson was released from the Woking Invalid Prison, effectively, to die. He passed away, unmourned, unmentioned, at 34 Harleyford Road, a shabby, busy street connecting Vauxhall and Brixton. He was 65.

***

A Curious Sequel: On New Year's Eve 1881, in Bucklesham, a small village near Ipswich, Suffolk, the rector, Rev. Mr. Walford, held his final services. A genial bee-keeping clergyman he was leaving to succeed his late father elsewhere. In February, it was announced that the Bucklesham living had been presented to the Rev. Samuel Roden Henderson, erstwhile curate of Batcombe. The new patron of the parish was, none other than, Miss Susanna Brown. She had purchased the benefice to reward Henderson for his faithful service in 1877.

Exactly what was the nature of the relationship between Susanna and her knight-errant? The reader shall be interested to know that Rev. Henderson had long been separated from his wife, including during his years in Batcombe. Once installed as the new rector of Bucklesham, Henderson enjoyed a splendid ivy-clad rectory, where Susanna, his patroness, frequently stayed as a "paying guest." It was a most curious arrangement and one that lasted for most of a decade. When the long absent first Mrs. Henderson finally died in 1891, Susanna – now 53 – married the Rev. Mr. Henderson only a few weeks later. Had Watson been aware of this "relationship" between

Susanna and the married Mr. Henderson? Had he appended it to the little list of "menaces" at his disposal? To have raised this point at his trial might have helped Watson's cause. He did not.

Alas, the idyllic happy-ending in a Suffolk village still eluded Susanna. The 1890's were a time of agricultural depression in rural Britain. Farmers and the farming economy slumped badly; tithes were unmet. In 1894, the Rev. Mr. Henderson was adjudged a bankrupt.[51] Apparently, one of the few fortunate creditors who received payment was Charlotte Watson. The other creditors demanded to know why "the favoured sister-in-law" got to the head of the line. There was no mention in any of the reporting on these dreary bankruptcy proceedings of the interesting lives of the two sisters, daughters of a country clergyman, and their relationships with the late, unlamented Rev. Richard Marsh Watson.

3. "A CLERICAL LOTHARIO"

A Scandal at Acton Green Church

Rev. D. Spink
Rev. T. Coby-Thomas.

The Euston Road was generally acclaimed to be "one of the dingiest thoroughfares in London."⁵² In the mid-afternoon, a well-dressed man and woman, seemingly more of the middle than upper classes, were walking east on the Euston Road. The pavement was thick with people and barrows stacked with one thing or another for sale. With three great railway termini within a quarter mile of each other, the Euston Road was always a chaotic scene. In the roadway, omnibuses, carts, hansoms and, in August 1898, even a few of the new horseless carriages vied for the space to creep forward. The massive railway hotels loomed over the scene but, as ever near the stations, with so many transients and bargain seekers, there were the cheaper lodging houses. Alas, many were of the most dubious reputation.

> Enmeshed in the Western Maze of the Underworld, there are the Upper, the Middle and the Lower hells. There is the Upper Hell of Piccadilly, there is the Middle Hell of the Tottenham Court Road and Oxford Street, and the Lower Hell of the Euston Road.[53]

The man and woman padded along; as a gentleman, he had offered her his arm and she had taken it. They halted finally in front of one terraced line of doorways. William Le Queux, a popular novelist of the period, described a similar visit to the area:

> Taking a taxi to the Euston Road, [he] made a thorough examination of the high shabby house with its smoke-grimed lace curtains, a place which bore over the fan-light the words "Private Hotel." In the broad light of day it looked a most dull, uninviting place; more so

even than its neighbours. There are many such hotels in the vicinity of Euston Station, and this seemed the most wretched of them all, for the windows had not been cleaned for many months, while the steps badly wanted scrubbing.[54]

Our non-fiction gentleman climbed the short steps and knocked sharply on the door. A window opened above and a woman barked down, "the other door!" At the proper portal, the vocal landlady greeted them. Peering at the gentleman incredulously, she noticed he had made no effort to hide the fact he was a clergyman, wearing the "dog collar" of the Church of England. "Why, you're a priest," she said. "Yes, I am,' he answered, 'but never you mind about that." Nor would she mind; in the competitive world around her, few questions were asked. Arrangements were made for a room for two hours. They were shown up to the first floor where there was a bedroom and a sitting room enlivened by the presence of a piano. It would be four shillings. The gentleman paid and the landlady returned below. "Let yourselves out,' she said in parting, 'you won't want to see me again."

The Rev. Turberville Cory-Thomas[55], for that was the grand name of this handsome clergyman, was 32 years old. He was a recently-arrived curate in the parish of St. Alban the Martyr in the west London suburb of Acton Green. His ecclesiastical career had been a varied and interesting one. He was born in Birmingham, of Welsh parents. His father was a copper agent. Turberville went out to

Canada after his father's death in 1877. He had hoped to serve with General Wolseley's forces in the British suppression of the Riel rebellion in Manitoba, but he was rejected as too young.[56] Turberville next went south into the United States where he studied and was ordained in the Anglican diocese of Chicago. At his first church in Wisconsin, he married a woman from his congregation; she died young, leaving him with two children. Placing the children with his late wife's family, he served briefly in Chicago where he won favourable notice as the preacher in the Anglican Church built to serve the English entourage at the 1893 World's Fair on the South Side. From there, he became the rector in a parish in Ishpeming a remote and frigid mining town on the Upper Peninsula of Michigan. There he was again popular (perhaps too much so with the ladies) and there was even talk of his standing for mayor. Nonetheless, in 1897, he decided to return to England.

Turberville arrived bearing letters of introduction from his two former American bishops, but he could only find employment with the Society for the Propagation of the Gospel in Foreign Parts (S.P.G.). This meant taking trains and coaches around England passing the hat for missionaries. A "powerful preacher with a mellow voice," he was quite good at his job. The message was simple: "Go forth and lift up the great cross of the world's Saviour." But his approach was different: "This gentleman's style is new to missionary meetings, which are not usually scenes with which one associates riotous mirth."[57] In late 1897, he was at last licensed by the Archbishop of Canterbury which meant he could hold church employment. He was still naught but a curate which meant any position would be temporary; he spent a very short time in Birkenhead, then came south to East Lavington in Sussex. It was there that he saw the advertisement in the *Church Time*s for a curate needed in the rapidly growing west London suburb of Acton Green.

St. Alban the Martyr, Acton Green.
Photo taken in 2012, courtesy of Dr. Neil Clifton.

The parish of St. Alban the Martyr was a just decade old. The new church of red brick held over 700 souls. The recently arrived vicar was the Rev. Bernard Spink whose task seemed a large one: "In his new position he will be called upon to carry on a herculean work on a small income, but as he is already in possession of private means the poverty of the benefice will be no barrier."[58] But, on the bright side, Mr. Spink would have a curate. In April, 1898, Mr. Cory-Thomas was interviewed, hired, and very quickly won the admiration and friendship of his vicar. The work was hard: daily services, four on Sunday, and the usual parochial rota of charities, fetes and sick-calls. In November of that year, the curate announced his engagement. Marriage was not generally recommended for curates but Mr. Cory-Thomas seemed to have made an excellent choice in Isabel Banks, a widow whose late husband had been a successful merchant in New Zealand. They met in Graffham, a village near Lavington, where he had made one of his brief stops. They were married on 10 January 1899 at St. Michael's, Chester Square in Belgravia. The ceremony was performed by the very posh society cleric, the Rev. Canon James Fleming who was assisted by Mr. Spink. The vicar of Acton Green declared himself well-pleased in his new curate, "I have never met a more conscientious & diligent worker and regard him as a personal friend."

That April, a few days after Easter, Mr. Spink was walking to Evensong when he was approached by one of the ladies who volunteered at St. Alban's. "Do you still trust Mr. Cory-Thomas?" the woman asked. "What do you mean by such a question?" the vicar replied. The story the woman told, in great emotion, shocked Spink greatly. He attempted to console her, urging her to calm down and then she must put her claims in writing. A few days later, he received her statement, which began, "What I am going to say to you now no one on earth knows except Mr. Cory-Thomas and myself, not even my sister." Of course, it involved that afternoon at the "hotel" in the Euston Road. Before and since that occasion, he had sought to seduce her. She had not surrendered all to him but "he did what he should not." Worse, he had tried much the same thing with her younger sister. The latter woman also stated in writing:

> He asked me to meet him in London and have lunch with him, and then proposed to me to go a hotel and spend the night with him. He said if he got me into trouble, he would take me to Rouen, and that if it came to the worst he would marry me. I know him to be a liar and a bad, wicked man. I could tell you many other things about him.

The furious vicar of Acton Green was confronted with what he called a "plot hatched in hell."

The women making these accusations against Cory-Thomas were unmarried sisters, residing with their mother in Acton. At no time were the women publicly identified by name; in all the news accounts and during the ensuing sensational trial, they were differentiated only by their respective ages – the older sister, the younger sister. The older sister was about forty and she shall henceforth be referred to as Miss O. The younger sister, or Miss Y, was thirty-five.[59]

It is worth repeating that when the Rev. Cory-Thomas arrived in Acton Green he was a widower. He lived alone in rooms in Chiswick. Early on, he met Miss O who was among the parochial volunteers at St. Alban's; in effect, she was a local missionary – a role that held special appeal for the new curate. She would visit families in need or in sickness, circulate literature and help with Sunday school and the like. Miss O's mother was elderly and unwell and could not get out. The new curate took to visiting the old lady regularly and quickly became a favourite, often enjoying tea with the woman and her two daughters, having also been introduced to Miss Y. A closeness between Miss O and the curate had blossomed and she considered herself to be in love with him.

In August 1898, Miss Y had to go into London to do some shopping prior to taking a summer holiday in Llandudno. Mr. Cory-Thomas, as it happened, was also going to be in London that day and they agreed to meet for lunch. He met her at Charing Cross and suggested they dine at Gatti's, the well-known restaurant at the foot of the Strand. She agreed. Lunch at Gatti's, what a treat! There was nothing like it in Acton Green. The "bustle and clatter," the waiters gliding past in their dress clothes and black ties, everyone sneaking a look hoping to see one of the reigning theatrical "demigods" make an appearance.[60] But according to Miss Y, during the meal, the Rev. Cory-Thomas actually suggested that she finish her tea and accompany him the short walk over to the Charing Cross Hotel where he would arrange for a lovely room for the two of them. He would have to run down and "take church" in Acton but he would come back to her for the night. Quite honestly, she could not believe what she was hearing and simply told him to "Stop being such a wicked man." She categorically refused to continue the conversation and the matter was dropped. Knowing her sister's affection for the curate, she chose not to tell Miss O. Nor did she tell her mother; it was all too outrageous. In Miss Y's case, this seems to have been a one-off venture on the part of the amorous Rev. Cory-Thomas.

A few days after dodging the Gatti's gambit, Miss Y went to Euston Station for her train to Llandudno. Miss O accompanied her. As the Acton ladies waited on the platform, who should appear but the Rev. Mr. Cory-Thomas. He could not allow Miss Y to go off without a farewell and his wishes for a safe journey. When the train smoked off for North Wales, the reverend gentleman turned to Miss O to ask whether she had had lunch. Off they went to dine in the Tottenham Court Road. Over lunch, Cory-Thomas proved more persuasive with the older of the sisters and Miss O agreed to accompany him to one of the "hotels" in the Euston Road. Miss O would never deny going willingly with Cory-Thomas though she knew it was wrong. As she explained in her statement to the vicar, "My life had been so hard that when he came and made love to me it seemed to brighten all my surroundings. I felt that in the midst of all the sorrow and pain I am going through in a hundred ways I must thank God for such a friend." But she resisted him nonetheless. In the grim bed-sit room, he told her how much he loved her. Wouldn't she like to take off her hat and coat? She demurred. She would not kiss him. She let him touch her improperly. They remained in the room for most of the paid-for two hours. He had become so emotional she was afraid that he might cause a great scene if she tried to leave. Finally, they left and returned to Acton separately.

The two sisters now each had a secret they did not share. Neither Miss O nor Miss Y had thought to inform the Rev. Spink of the clerical Lothario he had loosed upon St. Alban's parish. Why not, it should be asked. Miss O, in fact, continued to work beside the curate. Mr. Cory-Thomas continued to call at their home where the *mater* certainly remained in ignorance. On one afternoon, while in the kitchen seeing to the tea, Miss O was again importuned by the curate. She had always permitted him some little liberties, flirtatious hand squeezes, maybe a peck, perhaps more. But on that day, he suggested they go upstairs together, an outlandish proposal to be sure. She scolded him.

Then, in November, the news came that the Rev. Turberville Cory-Thomas was engaged. In the homes of the parishioners of St. Alban's, save one, undoubtedly, this romantic intelligence came as happy news. In Miss O's case, the blow was cushioned when the curate came to her to confess that it was a loveless arrangement. The betrothed was Mrs. Banks, a wealthy widow whose husband's

Antipodean fortune was made from shipping grains and frozen meat.[61] Cory-Thomas bemoaned his poverty, he was an underpaid curate still supporting his not forgotten children. He was "obliged" to marry this woman for her resources. No definitive statement can be made on the wealth in the sisters' family but it likely was modest. Oh, how he wished he was free to marry Miss O! Though greatly disappointed, the elder sister admitted that she could not control her feelings for him. She did not stop seeing him. "I can honestly say he did not live with me, because he did not. But he did what he should not." A few days before his wedding, she even went shopping with Cory-Thomas and bought him a new dressing gown as a present. It would be their secret. On his wedding day, Cory-Thomas contrived to be alone with Miss O and slipped a small ring on her finger, emblematic of his true feelings.

Now something obviously happened between that wedding day in January and April 1899 to despoil this love story. Clearly, at some point, Miss Y spilled her secret to her sister. Miss O was already miserable with nothing but her memories and forced to watch the Rev. and Mrs. Cory-Thomas go about the parish, with her daughter and Llewellyn, the curate's American son. Whether she was told accidentally or with cruel intent that her younger sister had been his first choice to seduce, it must have been a shattering moment. A few days after Easter, Miss O went to Rev. Spink. Per his request, each sister wrote out her story of the profligacy of Mr. Cory-Thomas.

Were these factual accounts or the lubricious creations of two giddy spinsters? That is the entire crux of this story. Rev. Spink clearly accepted their words. In fact, it is somewhat remarkable that, given the relationship that Mr. Spink had formed with his young curate, that the vicar was so quick to throw him over. Mr. Cory-Thomas was summoned to the vicarage and informed of his immediate dismissal. The vicar would say only that the gravest charges against his character had been made by two ladies of the parish. "Which ones?" the curate demanded. Spink was in disbelief, "Are there more?" When told it was "the sisters," Cory-Thomas tried to explain but was cut off. Instead, Spink went on, "You dogged the woman day after day and week after week with the object of ruining her. It was a plot hatched in hell." This was, of course, a private meeting between the two clergymen. Their versions, of course, would differ. In Spink's account, Cory-Thomas denied nothing and chose to beg for mercy. He agreed that he would have to go but, if a public scandal could be avoided, he might emigrate with his wife to New Zealand where her friends "have some influence with the Primate." Spink was obdurate throughout; he would do his best to ensure that Cory-Thomas never be allowed to serve the Church again, in England or anywhere. The disconsolate curate's final appeal was, "If you only knew how she tempted me, you would have some pity." The vicar erupted in fury, "Get out of my office before I throw you out!"

The vicar of Acton Green did as he had vowed to do: he immediately wrote to the Archbishop of Canterbury and to the offices of the S.P.G. He also sent letters to the Bishop of Chicago and the Bishop of Marquette, the diocese containing Cory-Thomas' old church in Ishpeming. This was a slow process, one in stark contrast with our day of instant reference checking. There was very little information sharing and the need for clergy so great that Cory-Thomas fairly soon found work in Norfolk. But Rev. Spink somehow heard of it, wrote immediately, and the services of the temporary curate were abruptly terminated.

There was a war on in South Africa and in January 1900 it was reported that Turberville Cory-Thomas, "of London, formerly of Pembrokeshire," had enlisted in the Imperial Yeomanry. Founded by the Lord Mayor of London, the I.Y. were the darlings of the City at the moment, sent off with great fanfare that May. Many of the officers were merchants or their sons; Cory-Thomas held only the rank of corporal in the 20th Battalion, the so-called "Rough Riders for [General] Buller."[62] They were modeled on the irregular forces led by the American Teddy Roosevelt in the recently concluded Spanish-American War. Cory-Thomas saw some service on the veldt but was invalided home for illness as opposed to wounds.

He returned to a nation in mourning. London was a city in black; crepe was everywhere. Queen Victoria had died on 22 January 1901, laid to rest almost a fortnight later at Frogmore beside her beloved

Albert. Long live the King; Edward VII was soon to give his name to a new era. The imperial capital was still filled with mourners, heads of state and representatives of Her late Majesty's empire from Perth to the Punjab. The newspapers, many of them still displaying the black borders of respect, were columned with accounts of the great funeral but also the numberless tributes and memorials being held in the cities, towns and shires across Britain. However, amidst all this glorious grief, the *New York Times* reported, "In strict accuracy, the subject that has been most gossiped about this week in London is the clerical libel suit."[63] Whilst Cory-Thomas was off at the war, a third woman had come forward to accuse him of misconduct. She was a temperance lecturer living apart from her husband. She was also never identified by name[64], thus, Mr. Cory-Thomas' three accusers were Miss O, Miss Y and Mrs. T. The case of *Cory-Thomas v. Spink* came on for trial at the Law Courts in the Strand on Wednesday, 6 February.

The case of the curate (the plaintiff) was in the hands of a fellow Welshman, John Eldon Bankes, a veteran attorney but newly minted K.C. He was a grandson of the famous jurist, Lord Eldon. Bankes told Lord Justice Bruce and the special jury empaneled that Mr. Cory-Thomas came before them not in pursuit of any financial damages from his former vicar but only the restoration of his good name so that he could resume his clerical career. That career had been closed when the defendant (Mr. Spink) had improperly and maliciously libeled him in a series of letters to Archbishops, Bishops and religious agencies – all based on false accusations made by, now, three jealous women. The lead counsel for the Rev. Spink was Sir Edward Clarke, in the eyes of many, the leading barrister of the day. Clarke was prepared to argue that the letters were both privileged (the vicar had a duty to write them and the recipients a right to know) and justified (the information alleged in the letters was true.)

Bankes opened the proceedings by calling the plaintiff. Standing in the witness box, the Rev. Cory-Thomas made a "fine figure of a man, with jet black hair and beard and a killing 'dagger' moustache." If he was, as alleged, a "lady-killer," he looked the part. The absence of his wife was rather unhelpful. To have her there, even if she did not testify, would have made a silent statement. The press coverage was intense, sketch artists were busy, but there seems to be no mention of Mrs. Cory-Thomas being present at any time.[65] Led through the biographical details of his life and career, Cory-Thomas proved a charming witness. The jurors learned that Ishpeming was the Indian word for heaven.[66] But once back in England, Cory-Thomas had been delighted to find employment as a curate at St. Alban's. He thought he had established an excellent relationship with his vicar and believed he was well-liked in the parish. He was shocked, then, when Rev. Spink chose to summarily dismiss him. He thought he had earned a chance to defend himself against such "malicious tittle-tattle." The vicar refused to hear anything from him and threw him out of the vicarage, following that up with a series of libelous letters. Unable to find any church employment as a result, Cory-Thomas had enlisted in the Imperial Yeomanry and while on medical leave, he had brought this action to clear his name. He "absolutely" denied the charges made by these three women.

Bankes then read "the Spink letters" to the court; the recipients had been Bishop McLaren of Chicago, Illinois, Bishop Mott-Williams of Marquette, Michigan, Mr. Kemp of the S.P.G. and the Rt. Rev. Edward Benson, the Archbishop of Canterbury. The Archbishop, by the way, was in court, afforded an elevated seat near the bench where he displayed that "grim, fixed expression he usually wears." Sir Edward Clarke objected to the admissibility of the letters to the American bishops – they were not within the jurisdiction of an English court. The plaintiff would have to take those letters elsewhere. The Lord Justice said he would have to agree but the letters to the S.P.G. and the Archbishop remained at issue. Spink had written to Archbishop Benson, who had promptly responded: "I will take care the monster never officiates again."

The cross-examination of the plaintiff took most of the first day of the trial. It began with a diversion. Since his return to England in 1897, on various occasions, Cory-Thomas had identified himself as "Doctor" Cory-Thomas, sometimes using the initials D.D., Doctor of Divinity. Clarke wanted to know more about this doctorate. It had been given to the clergyman by a Greek religious order. "Would that be 'The Chivalric and Religious Order of the Crown of Thorns'?" Clarke asked. It was and the Grand Master, Archbishop Vilatte[67], had been pleased to honour him, the witness replied. Reading the fulsome phraseology of the proclamation with all mock solemnity, Clarke wondered whether Cory-Thomas was entitled to be addressed as *Christianissimo*? He was but he did not use the title. Was he aware that his American bishop had called the degree, in effect, worthless? That was one man's opinion and the witness was gratified by the degree nonetheless.

The gratuitous aspersion upon Mr. Cory-Thomas' CV having been put out before the jury, Clarke called attention to the brief time the curate had served in Birkenhead. Had he been engaged to a woman in that town? He had. Clarke suggested that the woman's brother, being concerned, had gone to the local vicar who wrote to Mr. Cory-Thomas' former superiors in the United States. Clarke read from one of the replies: "Mr. Cory-Thomas, now passing as Dr. Cory-Thomas, does not enjoy my confidence." Had the engagement ended? The witness acknowledged that it had been broken off at the Birkenhead lady's request. As he was planning to leave the area, he did not press the issue. He went south to be a curate in Lavington where he met his present wife. They had not been engaged until sometime after he came to Acton Green. Not long between engagements, Clarke dared to suggest. Several months, the witness replied.

Clarke stated that the Rev. Spink would swear that during their meeting in April 1899, when confronted with these awful claims against him, the curate's first response was, "I deny nothing. I throw myself upon your mercy." In fact, Mr. Spink wrote those words down on an envelope. "I never made such a statement," Cory-Thomas insisted. It was true that he quickly suspected "the sisters" were involved. Miss O had "virtually proposed a marriage" from the day he came to St. Alban's. She very quickly became quite attached to him, contrived to be in his company and repeatedly asked him to marry her. He had been trying to dissuade her for some time. Was he, Clarke wanted to know, asking the jury to believe that the best way to end this unsought relationship was to invite the woman to an hourly "hotel" in the notorious Euston Road? Cory-Thomas explained that it had been his intention to speak with her during lunch in the Tottenham Court Road but there was no privacy and, as she was very emotional, he feared a scene. He went to the hotel only for privacy. But he rented a bedroom? A bedroom and a sitting room, and they never entered the former, he testified. What did they do for two hours, Clarke inquired. They had a long conversation but once his position was made clear to her, Miss O – according to Cory-Thomas – became angry and made threats. She would ruin him. Lots of tears were shed and it was some time before they were composed enough to depart. Cory-Thomas insisted that he never urged her to take her clothes off, never touched her, kissed her or asked her to go away with him on a holiday.

The curate's explanation of his relationship with Miss O, if not beyond challenge, was plausible. When Clarke raised the matter of Miss Y's luncheon at Gatti's, however, Cory-Thomas would only answer that he did not remember meeting her in London that day nor did he remember ever having lunch with her. Justice Bruce sought clarity. "You want the jury to take that as your answer, you do not remember?" The witness confirmed it. This is somewhat important. If he had not been there, why didn't he just flatly deny it? If he denied it, the other side would have to seek out a waiter or someone to identify Cory-Thomas and Miss Y as being there together. It was commonplace, of course, for waiters, compensated for "their time," to give such evidence. Still, a denial would have been better received than an "I don't remember."

Mrs. T, the late-arriving third accuser, now enters the account. Mr. Cory-Thomas admitted having first met her while working with the S.P.G. when both attended a temperance conference in Portsmouth. More recently, he had invited her to come to Acton to speak to the parish chapter of the Band of Hope, a youth group dedicated to battling "the evils of drink." When questioned by his own council as to Mrs. T's age, Cory-Thomas laughed, "She won't appreciate me for this, but she is nearly fifty." Never mind her age, Clarke declared, wasn't it true that Mrs. T was a married woman. She was but she lived apart from her husband. Cory-Thomas admitted meeting her in London on several occasions for lunch, "she was a friend of mine." Did he once come all the way from Birkenhead to meet her at Victoria Station and then travel by cab to a private hotel in Euston? He did remember such an occasion. It was a meeting to renew their friendship and mutual interests. He did not kiss her in the cab. There was a fire lit in the hotel bedroom, he did not specially request it. He did not behave improperly. He never told her that as she lived apart from her husband, there was no adultery involved in taking a lover. Had he asked for a bottle of whisky? He did not recall asking for one, but there was whisky in the room and they drank some.

> Clarke: You were temperance advocates? [Laughter]
>
> Cory-Watson: Perhaps you don't appreciate there are different kinds of temperance.
>
> Clarke: Never mind that. Let's talk of chastity.

The only other witness for the plaintiff was Francis Kemp, secretary of the S.P.G. He testified that Cory-Thomas had been a successful lecturer for some year or so but, upon the receipt of a letter from the Rev. Mr. Spink, his services had been discontinued.

The case for the vicar of Acton Green would begin on the second day. Rev. Bernard Spink took the witness stand in his own defense. He was 40, short-ish, balding, a Lincolnshire man by birth, and ordained in Durham. And he was a newlywed! Clearly, romance was in the air in Acton Green. In late 1900, with no mention in the newspapers, Rev. Spink had married Cicely Ainslie, an Irish-born widow with a six-year old daughter.[68] That seems odd but the information was not used in any way during the trial. Still, at the time Spink was dealing with the sisters, he was – same as Cory-Thomas – a single man. In the witness box, Spink told the story of being stopped on the way to Evensong and hearing the most horrible allegations against the curate with whom he had worked closely and considered a friend. When the ladies, the "sisters," put their claims in writing, he resolved that Mr. Cory-Thomas would have to go immediately. On 24 April 1899 he informed his curate that "I will take care that you will never officiate as a clergyman again." The man's first reaction was to say, "I deny nothing." He asked to be quietly allowed to emigrate to New Zealand. Spink refused to be part of any "act." Cory-Thomas, became defiant and said he would "face it out," adding "I will show to you and to the world at large that my wife will stick to me." At that moment, if the jurymen and the crowded galleries turned to look for the face of Mrs. Cory-Thomas somewhere in the courtroom, they were disappointed. So much for "sticking" around.

The task for Bankes was to convince the jury that his client (Cory-Thomas) had been the victim of a sisterly plot, crafted to get revenge for the curate's marriage to Mrs. Banks. Rev. Spink had been quick to accept without question these accusations against his curate. He acknowledged that he took the charges seriously from the first. The vicar admitted that his former opinion of his curate had been quite good and there were no other complaints or rumours outstanding.[69] The vicar conceded that when the events in question took place, i.e. the Gatti's lunch and the Euston Road confab, Mr. Cory-Thomas was a single man, a widower. He was certainly allowed to associate or even "walk out" with women. Was Mr. Spink perhaps so unworldly that he could not understand that the course of modern love "never did run smooth?" Spink agreed that feelings could be quite easily hurt in such matters. Bankes wondered whether the vicar had ever considered Miss O to be at all vindictive. In her letter to Rev. Spink, Miss O had coldly dismissed any pain that these charges might bring to Mrs. Cory-Thomas. "She went into it with her eyes open," Miss O wrote. The vicar said he could not comment on anyone's motivation.

> Bankes: Is your experience as a man sufficient to know that a jealous woman is a dangerous woman?
>
> Spink: I know that.
>
> Bankes: Was "the elder sister" not an extremely jealous woman?
>
> Spink: Her letters did not trouble me.
>
> Bankes: Did she address you as her "dearest and most trusted friend?"
>
> Spink: Yes.

> Bankes: She also wrote that you had been very kind to her. You are a married man, aren't you, Mr. Spink? [NB: Spink was a married man, however, he was not at the time he first heard the charges from Miss O.]
>
> Spink: (warmly) I won't allow the learned counsel to suggest anything of the kind.

The question was objected to and Bankes agreed to move on. He asked the vicar about Mrs. T – the temperance lady. When she first came to Mr. Spink with her story, hadn't she mentioned how much she resented "the new Mrs. Cory-Thomas and her airs?" Mrs. T was another very jealous woman, was she not? Wasn't it wrong, Bankes asked the clerical witness, for a married woman (Mrs. T) to agree to come to London and then retire to a private hotel with a man not her husband? Mr. Spink admitted as much. And wasn't it just as wrong for Miss O, knowing that Cory-Thomas was engaged to wed another, to continue to seek his society, engage in little liberties and buy him secret presents? It was not proper conduct, Spink again conceded. As a clergyman and in his role as spiritual advisor in St. Alban's, had he ever spoken with either woman on their relations with his curate? Not specifically, the vicar replied.

When Mr. Spink left the witness box, Sir Edward Clarke rose to ask for a judgement from the bench. He thought that the plaintiff's case had totally fallen to the ground. It was unfortunate that Mr. Cory-Thomas was still trying to blame his accusers rather than take the responsibility for his actions.

Clarke insisted that his only wish was to spare these three women from a distasteful public ordeal. As for the Rev. Spink, he had only communicated to those men who needed to have this information. What he reported to them was true. "M'lord, there is no case to answer," Clarke asserted and requested a dismissal. Justice Bruce, "a typical jurist of the old Vanity Fair school," looked down with his sunken eyes and declined, "I cannot do that, Sir Edward, call your witnesses."

A heavily veiled figure entered the witness box. A slip of paper was handed up to the bench with the woman's name on it. Miss Y was then sworn and told she would be required to raise her veil.[70] Clarke asked Justice Bruce to insure that all the sketch artists had been removed and no likenesses be made by anyone in court. The instructions were given. History is left to rely on the descriptive prose talents among the pressmen. Little was written about Miss Y other than that she was a woman in her mid-thirties. It was reported that neither sister was particularly "fetching." She described the day in August 1898 when, by mutual agreement, she met "the plaintiff" in Charing Cross sometime after one p.m. They lunched at Gatti's and during the meal he proposed staying the night at the Charing Cross hotel. "He would go down to Acton, take the evening service, and come back to me." She turned to his Lordship on the bench, "Must I say all?" She must. Miss Y stated that the curate promised that, if necessary, he would take care of her and marry her. She told him he was a wicked man with no right to make such a disgusting proposal. Perhaps he could find another woman among all the St. Alban's ladies who fancied him. When they left Gatti's, he walked away up St. Martin's Lane. While away in Llandudno, she wrote to him, asking that he keep away from her home. When she had returned to London, Cory-Thomas came round nonetheless; he told her he didn't appreciate her "preaching" tone. Then, he said, "Remember, whatever game I play, whoever loses, I win." Miss Y, knowing Miss O's attachment to Mr. Cory-Thomas, resolved not to tell her sister. But, early in 1899, she was planning to move away from Acton and decided she could not leave her sister alone if she did not know the truth about this man.

The suit was being heard by a "special jury" – made up of men from the professional and merchant classes, presumably somewhat sophisticated. But everyone in London knew of Gatti's.

> Tragedies and comedies have been enacted over those marble-topped tables, which, if they were related, would make the fortune of a thousand playwrights.[71]

It would have been extremely crowded at lunchtime, Mr. Bankes suggested as he cross-examined Miss Y. Would it be at all the setting to make such a shocking, intimate suggestion to a lady? She assured him that it had happened. Why didn't she just get up and leave if the proposal disgusted her? She chose to finish her meal. Did she really suggest that Mr. Cory-Thomas take his disgusting proposal to another lady at the church? Was that her idea of a joke? Perhaps she thought Mr. Cory-Thomas was merely joking? "He looked very serious at the time," she recalled. Why hadn't she gone straight home and told her mother? "It would have killed her." Of course, the central question was why she kept this secret from her sister for eight months. She was well aware of her sister's passionate interest in Mr. Cory-Thomas. "She told me that she loved him." Miss Y seemed to imply a hint of disapproval of her older sister's relations with the curate. When Miss O and Cory-Thomas would playfully tease one another, Miss Y testified that she "would have to leave the room until they were finished." And yet, she said nothing to her sister about Cory-Thomas' proposal? "I never tell anything about what happens to me," Miss Y responded firmly. But Bankes suggested that, by her silence, she permitted this "wicked" man to enter her home and continue to enjoy the society of her mother and sister. "I didn't think he was so bad but I knew he was wrong at the time."

Miss O's turn in the witness box was held over into the third day. We are favoured with a slightly more detailed description of her: she was about forty with a pallid complexion, strongly marked features and bright eyes. Miss O testified to meeting Cory-Thomas during her work at St. Alban's and he, not she, had initiated their special friendship. He had flattered her: she was "a woman after his own heart and so on." Later, he embraced and kissed her, declaring they were "one in spirit" and he would marry her if he could but he was engaged. [The timing here causes some confusion. The Birkenhead engagement had ended before this time – pre-August 1898. His engagement to Mrs. Banks was not announced until November 1898. He knew Mrs. Banks prior to his days in Acton so it is possible that he considered himself engaged to the New Zealand woman, pending some formalities.] But, he had assured Miss O, it was a cold engagement. Clarke asked if Miss O had ever proposed marriage to Cory-Thomas? "Never," she answered. On the day they saw Miss Y off from Euston, she and Cory-Thomas had lunch in the Tottenham Court road. Afterwards, he asked her, "Will you come and have a rest at a quiet place?" She consented to go with him. They went to a place called "Crescent House," with a small sign in the window. The woman who greeted them said, "You are a priest." Cory-Thomas replied, "Yes I am, never mind about that." Once in the sitting room, he asked Miss O to remove her hat and coat. She only removed her hat. He then began to "misbehave," but the details were considered unfit for publication. She struggled free which angered him. He complained, "I am a starving child and you only give me half a loaf." Miss O claimed not to take his meaning. After leaving the room, they took separate omnibuses home. As her sister had before her, Miss O told no one. Still, the curate continued to be admitted to her home. On a subsequent visit, he apologised for his actions in Euston. He loved her so much he had forgotten himself. She forgave him and their friendship resumed. This clearly involved kissing and hugging, what one newspaper called "canoodling."[72] But again he wanted more, he begged her to be his mistress. She refused him. Miss O told Clarke that she first heard of her sister's Gatti's encounter with Cory-Thomas at Easter 1899 and she went to the Rev. Mr. Spink three or four days later.

"How old are you, may I ask," Mr. Bankes began by way of cross-examination. Miss O was 39. Had she written many letters to Mr. Cory-Thomas? She thought perhaps a dozen. Bankes implied there were many more than that. "Were they in the nature of love-letters?" he asked. Some, she agreed. Miss O admitted that she had not been a church volunteer until after the new curate had arrived in the parish. Contrary to her earlier testimony, she now admitted that she introduced herself to him in June 1898. Had not Mr. Cory-Thomas told her from the first that he was engaged? He had. Did she not realise it was "a discreditable thing" for a woman to allow a man engaged to be married to make love to her? Not at first, she said. Bankes wanted to know what "innocent purpose" she had in mind when she agreed to go with an engaged man to a lodging house bedroom. "A quiet talk" is what she expected. They remained in the room for more than an hour. Could she explain why, if Mr. Cory-Thomas had acted in the way she described, she didn't leave immediately? He was in such a foul temper, she feared a scene. In fact, wasn't it true that the curate left the room for five minutes (for the loo?) and still she remained? She did not deny it. There was a piano in the room, did she play it? Possibly. She was not so fearful that she could not play the piano! In her original statement to Mr. Spink she asserted that Mr. Cory-Thomas' conduct in that Euston bed-sit made him unfit to be a clergyman and unfit for the company of any decent woman. Yet, even after that afternoon, she allowed him to visit her mother's home. After some sort of an apology, she even let this engaged man resume taking little liberties, hand-holding, hugs and kisses. She even bought him a wedding present. No, she insisted, the dressing robe was solely a "friendship gift." Could she explain her conduct? Barely audible, and choking back a sob, Miss O admitted: "I loved him and if he is really sorry I should say, 'Yes, he is fit to associate with any decent woman!'" Wasn't it true that it was only after his marriage that she thought to raise questions about his conduct? "Yes, I did not think he had behaved very badly to me until he married someone else. Then I felt I could not believe in him, and I told Mr. Spink of the matter." Reading from her statement to the vicar, Bankes quoted, "I do not think [Cory-Thomas] should be allowed to go out of the parish without being shown up in one way or another...Nothing will do but to bring down his pride and self-conceit." Was she motivated by her concern for a clergyman's fitness or her own jealousy? Hadn't she beseeched the vicar to publicly humiliate the curate, while keeping her out of it? She had written to Mr. Spink, "I do not think you need to mention names or go into details." Her plan had not worked, Bankes concluded, "you realised in your endeavour to show up [Cory-Thomas], you had involved yourself."

Together, the Misses O and Y had spent the better part of two days under questioning. They were easily ridiculed as "very giddy... and far too innocent of this wicked world to be allowed to stray far from mother's apron strings." Nonetheless, they maintained their composure in the face of Bankes' lengthy examinations. Miss O especially had behaved "very bravely." The "sisters" had made their case against Cory-Thomas. Mrs. T was to follow. She was described as a "stout woman wearing furs" and appearing to be nearer fifty than forty years old. As the clerk approached the box to swear in the new witness, the foreman of the jury rose to say that there was no need for any further evidence. In his seat, the Rev. Cory-Thomas bowed his head.

Sir Edward Clarke would give the first closing statement. It was brief and had, in parts, the tone almost of a victory speech. He thanked "his learned friend" [Mr. Bankes] for the "delicate, courteous and able manner" in which he had conducted the case for the plaintiff. However, the defendant, Mr. Spink, clearly deserved the verdict. He had done no more than his simple duty to report his curate's conduct to the Archbishop, who had licensed him, and the S.P.G., which had employed him. He was confident the jury would agree as to Mr. Cory-Thomas unfitness to be a clergyman. They would show by their verdict that he had been "guilty of an attempt to demoralize and seduce two ladies whose position ought to have secured them from it, even if his priestly office had not prevented him from attempting so great a crime."

According to the "European correspondent" of *The New York Herald*, "From the moment Sir Edward Clarke sat down after his closing statement, the verdict was never in doubt." Still, Mr. Bankes would have his say. He began by acknowledging that the jury's earlier statement had left him in a rather difficult position. His client, Mr. Cory-Thomas, had come before them because "all that made his life endurable" was at stake. Putting the question of privilege aside, were the stories told by these two women true? "Wasn't it possible that Mr. Spink allowed himself to be duped by these two women, particularly by Miss O, women who made him their weapon to attack the Rev. Cory-Thomas?" Certainly, it was a regrettable decision by the curate to bring Miss O to that room in the Euston Road. But the fact that he felt the need to have a serious, private conversation with the woman was certainly a possible, nay probable, explanation. Did she vow to never see him again? Hardly, in fact, he was back in her home where she flirted with him so much, Miss Y had to leave the room in disgust. As for the Charing Cross incident, who in their senses could believe Miss Y kept this secret locked within her bosom for eight months? It was released only after the curate's marriage, when the elder sister, with jealous vindictiveness, determined to "blast the life out of this man." By their decision, the jury would determine whether Mr. Cory-Thomas left the Royal Courts worthy of the honour and respect of his friends, or as a social leper and outcast. It was up to them: were these women telling the truth, yes or no?

Whatever hope there might have been at the plaintiff's table in that courtroom, it was short-lived. Taking less than a quarter hour, the jury returned a verdict: "We find the charges are true in substance and in fact, and that Mr. Spink honestly believed them to be true. We find for the defendant." There were shouts and some applause at the verdict, ineffectually suppressed by Justice Bruce, whose instructions to the jury - delivered in a dull monotone - had been quite tilted to the vicar's case over the curate's. The victorious Mr. Spink "beamed visibly" but surely not out of relief. The decision could hardly have been called a surprise. Mr. Bankes' closing speech - according to one reporter - had "elicited ill-concealed sneers from the jury box." *The Pall Mall Gazette* called the denouement "a foregone conclusion, barring the improbable hypothesis that the jury box would be filled with a dozen driveling idiots in the place of the average species of 'good men and true.'"

The Rev. Mr. Cory-Thomas, appearing gray and pale, had shown no emotion, staring ahead. If not a literal outcast, he had no chance of church employment and faced a large legal bill (each side was left to pay their costs). He issued a written statement:

> I am not discouraged. My conscience is clear. I have my health to begin life anew. Since I worked myself through college as a poor boy, fought my way through the university, got my degree in Milwaukee, and was ordained, I have never known what it is to be discouraged ... As an American, it is surprising to me to learn that a British jury will condemn a man on unsupported evidence. Two disappointed spinsters, who, as my counsel said, set their cap at a curate, brought these infamous charges against me only after I was married.

While claiming to be an American, Cory-Thomas soon put back on the King's khaki and there were reports he would be rejoining the British forces in South Africa. In his second stint on the veldt, Cory-Thomas earned a commission and was "mentioned in the dispatches." After the war, he and his son recrossed the Atlantic to settle in Alberta, in the Canadian Rockies. Mrs. Cory-Thomas did not accompany him thither; she and her daughter returned to Christchurch in New Zealand.[73] She did not divorce him: flirtations and failed seductions did not rise to the grounds required to prove adultery. But, curiously, she kept his name. What would it have mattered in New Zealand? In Canada, Cory-Thomas exchanged the pulpit for the saddle. He became a rancher. By 1906, he was in the newspaper business, editing papers in Camrose, Alberta, and later in Vancouver, British Columbia. He was 55 when he died of heart disease in Vancouver.[74]

The Rev. Mr. Spink was much congratulated by his friends and by most of the greater public. Through his courage and prompt actions, a "Don Juan" of the clergy had been exposed. But at great personal expense. The vicar's legal debts were in excess of £600 – multiply by forty, minimum, for today's equivalent. A public campaign was announced to raise funds to meet those costs; the Archbishop of Canterbury was gracious enough to seed the effort with a (rather chary) contribution of £50.[75]

As for the "sisters," they were to be pitied more than ridiculed. As church ladies, they should have heeded the warning of St. Paul, in his epistle to Timothy, to beware of men who "creep into houses and lead captive silly women."[76] Their morality was publicly questioned. Miss O and Miss Y had "some very peculiar ideas as to how they should treat a man who attempted to tamper with their most precious possession." Still, their identities had been protected. Questions were asked in the House of Commons about the fairness of suppressing their names. The Attorney General, Sir Robert Finlay, reminded the questioner that the arrangement had been reached by both sides in the matter with "the very proper object of avoiding the infliction of un-necessary pain and annoyance." Certainly, the prospect of nameless women being allowed to reveal their secrets from the witness box was not a pleasant prospect for more than a few "gentlemen."

Around London, across Britain, people wondered why Cory-Thomas ever brought this lawsuit. The "sheer sublime impudence" of the man. The seductive charmer of novel and stage was a Victorian cliché. Of course, what passes for roguish charm in some men is generally deplored in clergymen. If it was true that Miss O had "set her cap" on the new curate, it was not uncommon.

> [The curate] is left, therefore, largely to the mercies of certain elderly spinsters who seem drawn by some strange fascination to meddle in church work. Having no families of their own to look after, they endeavour to help other people to mind theirs. They consider the clergy fair game.[77]

But to argue that he deserved some merciful consideration for running across two susceptible spinsters who fell too hard for his "canoodling" banter was never going to find a favourable audience. Clergymen were not meant to be the subjects of "malicious tittle-tattle." They were expected to be on their best behaviour at all times.

> Wherever he is, at whatever hour, he must exemplify those qualities which in church he prays may be implanted in us all. Of no finer

> clay than we are, he must appear to be always gentle, cheerful, high-minded, simple-hearted, fulfilled with universal sympathy and love. He must behave, in fact, as a saint. Now, saints are rare, and not all of them are put into holy orders. Consequently, the number of really impressive curates is quite infinitesimal, and the number of really ridiculous curates is quite enormous.[78]

A few weeks after the trial, the editor of the society weekly, *Truth*, reported "one of the most pathetic letters that I have received for a long time," apropos of Turberville Cory-Thomas.

> The writer was a lady. I surmise a maiden lady. Her theme was the desolate condition of the "unwanted" maidens of the present day and the competition among the marriageable for husbands, as exemplified in the hunting of curates, even curates of such questionable character as the Rev. Turberville Cory-Thomas.[79]

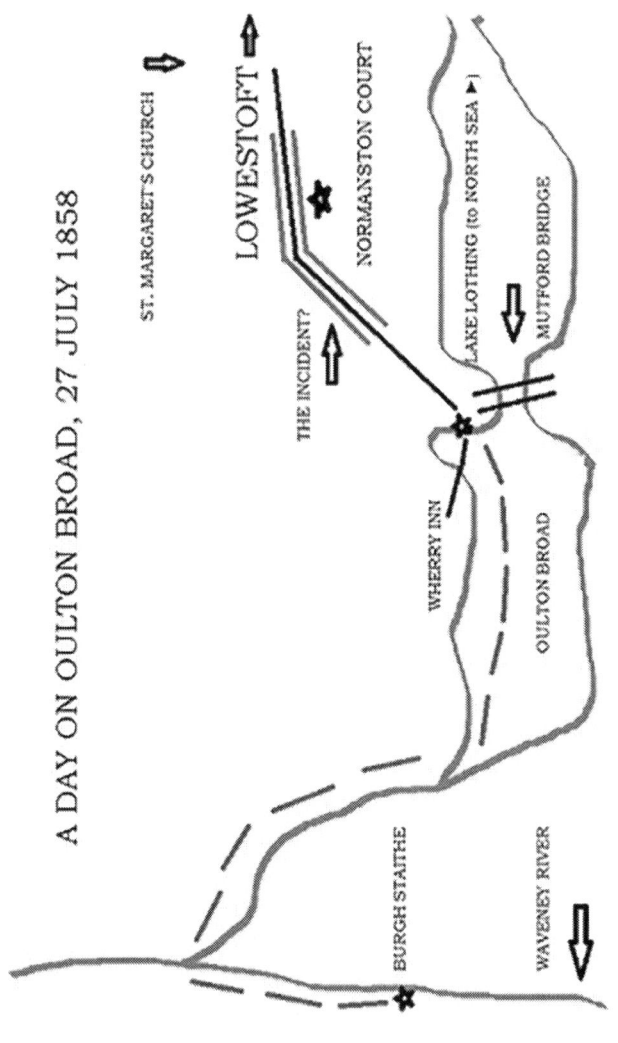

4. I'LL DO FOR DICKY RODGERS

The Rev. Edward Rodgers, Curate of Lowestoft

Oulton Broad[80] was "the water playground" of Victorian Lowestoft. Overshadowed, perhaps, by the larger and better-known Norfolk Broads, Oulton, which is in Suffolk, is nevertheless "a fine sheet of water." Mutford Bridge divides the fresh waters of the Broads to the west from the salt waters of "Lake" Lothing to the east. The latter leads out to the North Sea, a mile-and-a-half distant at Lowestoft. Circa 1858, at Mutford Bridge, the thirsty traveler would discover the *Wherry Inn*, where "parties may at all times procure boats either for fresh or salt water fishing or for pleasure." One sunny day that certain summer, the Rev. Edward Rodgers, curate of St. Margaret's, Lowestoft, set off from the *Wherry* for a jolly picnic cruise with some local youths. By nightfall, his reputation had been ruined.

The Rev. Mr. Rodgers[81] was 37. Born in Gateshead, raised in Newcastle, he'd trained for the clergy at St. Aidan's in the northern cathedral city of Durham. He was ordained in 1852. He had been a curate in Lowestoft for nearly six years. He and his wife, Mary Jane, were married in Wandsworth in 1854 and had a son, not quite two years old. The little lad, William Cunningham Rodgers, had been so named to honor the venerable vicar of St. Margaret's, the Rev. Francis Cunningham who had been a parson in and around Lowestoft since 1810. Rodgers was one of two curates at the large church. In addition to his liturgical duties, he also "looked in" at the local school. More than 100 boys – from the "necessitous classes," usually the sons of herring fishermen, attended the school, some free and some paying 1s per quarter. In fact, Mr. Rodgers had arranged the outing on Oulton Broad as a summer treat for the young scholars. To help shepherd the party, Rodgers had recruited 18-year old George Rix, one of the "pupil-teachers." George had previously made plans of his own for that day, hoping to go to Yarmouth. Although not without a grumble or two, George bowed to the curate's request.

Tuesday, 27 July 1858 was a very hot day in what had been a very hot summer. The mercury had recently broken 100° in Kent, setting an unofficial record for England that still stands. The Rev. Mr. Rodgers had a wedding to perform that morning and thus the plan was for everyone to meet at Mutford Bridge at noon. In all, counting the curate, the headmaster, Mr. Pratt, the schoolboys, George Rix and two or three other young men from Lowestoft who'd come along for the fun, there were 27 souls present when the cry was heard: "To the Boats."

The Wherry Inn (circa 1890)
Courtesy of Broadland Memories

Two wherries had been hired and provisioned for the event. Purpose built for the Broads, these flat-bottomed sailing vessels were easily mastered. "Two men, or a man and a boy, or his wife, or even one man only, suffice to navigate these large craft. They sail fast, very close to the wind, and are handy." Should the breeze falter, a quant would be employed, in a technique akin to punting on the Cam.[82] The planned itinerary for the day's outing was to cross Oulton Broad to the narrow channel of Oulton Dyke which flows north to meet the Waveney River. The Victorian author-angler Henry Cholmondeley-Pennell wrote, "From Oulton Dyke, the Waveney up to Beccles is a splendid river, broad, deep and clear." True but the Lowestoft party chose not to go all that way (six miles) upriver to the market town but rather they were planning go roughly half-way, nearly three miles, putting in at a place called Burgh Staithe (wharf), steering towards the curiously stepped tower of nearby St. Mary's church, a local landmark.

Reaching the staithe, some of the boys went ashore to play a rather unruly game of cricket whilst the older members of the party made their way straight for the *Waveney Inn* for "refreshments." Then, it was a late lunch – or early tea – of a cold joint, some breads and cheeses, and enjoyed by all. Mr. Rodgers and the headmaster got everyone back into their separate boats for what should have been a much quicker return downstream to Mutford. Alas, the strong drink from the inn had a predictable effect; poor George Rix got sick in the curate's boat and was good naturedly chaffed for it --- more good naturedly, of course, by those who were happy to be in the other boat. Then one of the children aboard Rodgers' wherry – as one will always do – fell overboard. There were a few anxious moments but the feckless lad, Henderson by name, was pulled from the river, drenched and inconsolable. Rodgers shouted to those in the other boat to head back alone while he took the second wherry back to the staithe to deal with the twin calamities.

The curate's boat did not return to Mutford Bridge until about seven p.m. The youngsters were quickly sent scampering back to their homes and to presumably their somewhat fretful parents. One or two of the adults aboard the first boat had been waiting at the *Wherry* and the Rev. Rodgers, Rix and a few others joined them to partake of the hospitality of the publican, Isaac Beaumont. Who drank what and how much would be a subject for subsequent dispute. But it was generally agreed that a convivial session was enjoyed at the inn, with glasses raised, many pipes lit and hearty tales shared of the events of a long day on Oulton Broad.

The merry-makers still faced a long walk from the inn, north into Lowestoft, much of it uphill. It was even longer for Mr. Rodgers going by way of St. Margaret's. The guidebooks described the old church as "inconveniently situated"[83] about a half-mile inland from the town. Those who had built the church, those hundreds of years before, had apparently feared that the North Sea would eventually take a great bite out of that part of the coastline. In fact, the waters had receded a good deal over time. Hence, St. Margaret's was happily safe and dry and the proud center of a thriving parish, but it was just that nettling bit "out of the way."

It was well past nine, when the last members of the boating party left the *Wherry*. As it is of some importance, we shall name them all: the Rev. Mr. Rodgers, young George Rix, Peter Barrett, the church sexton and bellman, Robert Whincup, a plumber and glazier, and William Moss, who kept the lower of Lowestoft's two seaside lighthouses. It had been a tiring day for all. It was still quite warm. Darkness was finally setting in on a midsummer's night. Soon after they had left the pub, Rev. Rodgers confided to Whincup, "Robert, my head is feeling very bad." The curate said he felt uncommon queer and was having trouble walking. He began to lag well behind the others on the path. Moss asked if the curate needed any help but Rodgers said, "Thank you, Moss, but I'm sure George will lend me his arm." Rix, the "pupil-teacher," lent his support to the clergyman but the two of them could not keep up with the other three. Barrett, Moss and Whincup continued on ahead.

The road back to the town passed Normanston Court, the seat of a local grandee, Edward Leathes. Normanston Park was "embosomed in trees" and the path took the walker between rising hedgerows on both sides. The trio of walkers, reaching the clearing beyond, decided to wait for the stragglers. A few minutes passed and Rix came into view with the unsteady curate following unaided. Moss again offered to assist and this time Rodgers accepted his arm and walked with him the rest of the way into Lowestoft. Rix, meanwhile, joined Peter Barrett and he was soon deep in quiet conversation with the church sexton. Soon, the two were sharing a raucous laugh and Whincup, who was nearby, would later swear that he heard Rix telling Barrett, "I suppose he thought I was his wife." Rodgers, meantime, looking more and more ashen and unwell, said nothing the rest of the way. The five men parted at a place called Three-corner Green. Rodgers was able to trudge the final steps to his rooms where he was greeted by his aforementioned wife.

The clergyman immediately collapsed on his couch and remained there for almost two hours. Mrs. Rodgers was finally able to rouse him, gave him some brandy-and-soda and helped him to his bed. Neighbours on the High Street recalled hearing his groans during the night. In the morning, Dr. Meadows was sent for. The local surgeon examined the patient and pronounced him the victim of "over excitement" and prescribed a regimen of opium draughts. Meadows ordered that Rev. Rodgers have absolute quiet and bed rest for at least two more days.

It was therefore Friday of that July week before the Rev. Rodgers was strong enough to rise from his sickbed. While he had been privately recuperating, others in Lowestoft were keenly discussing the question of the hour, "What, if anything, had happened in that darkened lane?" Only two men truly knew, of course, the Rev. Edward Rodgers and George Rix. And, in the end, they would tell two completely contradictory stories.

* * *

According to George Rix, on the first day that the Rev. Mr. Rodgers was able to leave his sick bed, he "looked in" at the school. George agreed to take a walk with the curate on the Denes, the beach at Lowestoft. During their walk, Rix insisted that the curate pleaded with his young assistant not to tell anyone what had happened that night. George would swear that Mr. Rodgers was in tears and said he was very sorry for what he had done that evening, actions he blamed on a combination of having more to drink than normal and being over-tired and over-heated. The curate insisted that he was prone to having "spells" and – after such an exhausting day - he had undergone a kind of mental attack. He offered to pray with Rix for the strength not to repeat his actions and beseeched the younger man to keep the story a secret between them. Rix agreed that he would keep silent.

But Rix – whether he ever made such a promise or not – had already told several people – in varying degrees of detail – *his version* of the incident in the lane. Barrett, Whincup and Moss all knew. And so did Charley Trigg, another of the pupil-teachers at the school. Trigg had heard the gossip from some of the adults in town and went to Rix for details. Rix had told him "you don't want to know." But Trigg persisted until Rix told him his story but then he made Charley vow not to tell another soul. This is quite plainly no way to keep a secret in Lowestoft.

As mentioned, it is important to differentiate Rix's account from the narrative told by the Rev. Rodgers. The clergyman recalled that his bilious attack lasted for two days before he could fully return to his duties. He had most definitely not gone immediately to see George Rix to review the events of the picnic. Any contact with George had solely to do with school affairs. In fact, Rodgers had no indication that he was the subject of any ribald comment until some weeks later, in Lowestoft. The curate went into the shop of a man named Adderton[84]. The shopkeeper seemed very cold towards him and the clergyman asked if he had done anything to offend. Adderton said he had heard a very troubling story about the curate's conduct which he would not repeat. When pressed, the shopkeeper said the story was that the curate had been reeling drunk on the Broads that day and that there had been "other irregularities." Certainly the latter was a phrase used for press censorship and not the shopkeeper's term. Adderton said he'd heard this tale from a lad named Cullingford, a joiner's assistant. But the shopkeeper also said "Rix knows all about it." Rodgers was understandably shaken by this development and, never strong, he again suffered some sort of collapse. George Rix had to be the source of this gossip and he summoned the young man to his home. In the curate's sick-room, Rix admitted he had been talking about the events that night on the walk back to Lowestoft. Rodgers demanded to know why George was saying any of this when he knew it was all untrue. The curate insisted that he had not been drunk but seriously unwell that night and clung to Rix purely for assistance while walking and nothing more. Nonetheless, within days of learning of this gossip and how far it had been circulated, Mr. Rodgers arranged to take leave and visit his family in London. It was too late.

Inevitably, all this talk would reach the ears of the vicar of Lowestoft. In March of 1859, several months having passed since the events of the picnic, the Rev. Cunningham wrote to Mr. Rodgers in London. Interestingly, the vicar first wrote asking for an answer only to the charge that his curate had been staggering drunk that day on the

Broads when he had chaperoned several children of the parish. There was no mention of any indecent conduct. However, in a second letter to his curate, dated the 5th of April, Cunningham reported that he had since been apprised of, once again euphemistically called, "additional irregularities." The vicar said there was talk that an indecent assault had been attempted or committed by the curate. Whether true or not, the rumour had attained wide circulation in Lowestoft. "Even the women talk of it," Cunningham fretted. The vicar was sorry to report, "I fear that I should stand alone if I were to say that I do not believe it." The best strategy, Cunningham proposed, was to allow his curate (Rodgers) to quietly resign.

> Your guilt has, I fear, been too publicly made known in this parish ... Now that you are quietly gone, I think that you had better remain away. I think that your return would make the whole affair burst into a blaze, whilst now it is only a smouldering fire, which may, I trust, not rise up to public observation. Your wife might return (if she could bear to do so) to pack up your furniture. ... I grieve for you, your wife, for Willy and for ourselves, and our ark, which will, I trust, be untarnished."

From Holloway, where Rodgers was staying with his brother, the curate replied immediately. He complained to Cunningham that after having given the parish so many years of blameless service, it was painful to learn that he had been found guilty without a chance to defend himself. "All I can do is assert my innocence in the face of your preconceived notions and in opposition to those who have maliciously set about the story." Rodgers admitted that his wife was "quite prostrated" over the matter. Nonetheless, "she thinks we had better go at once to Lowestoft as remaining here only prolongs our unhappiness and anxiety."

But, again, the vicar tried to convince Rodgers to stay away. You must be very cautious, he advised. More and more details were emerging. Cunningham now revealed that it was being said that Rix, on that evening, had actually shown the others (Moss, Whincup and Barrett) "his soiled clothes." Rix had also told several people that Rodgers had pleaded for forgiveness and silence, explaining that he had acted in a "state of craziness." According to the young man's account, he had pledged to keep Rodgers' secret and had not even mentioned it to his father. (Perhaps the only man in town not in on the scandal.) Poor Rev. Cunningham was ill equipped to deal with such matters but, as he wrote to Rodgers, it seemed impossible to believe that Rix could have invented such a horrible tale.

The new allegations and the disgusting detail of the charge hit Rodgers "like an electric shock." Too distraught to reply, Rodgers allowed his brother to answer for him. John Rodgers informed the vicar that as soon as Edward had the strength, he would return to Lowestoft to confront this "malicious slander." It would be at no small risk, John wrote, as there could be no proof either way and "people are so ready to believe evil."

The curate and Mrs. Rodgers did return to Lowestoft in July when the Rev. Cunningham conducted a private inquiry. It was an entirely extra-legal proceeding, there was no counsel permitted. By then, almost a full calendar year had passed since the outing. The vicar interviewed almost every person who had been on the picnic. Many interviewees remembered the curate's stumbling condition and there was a clear consensus that, at the very least, he appeared to be drunk. Rodgers, given his chance to speak, admitted to drinking some beer and brandy that day but blamed his stumbling gait on exhaustion, the day's heat and being sickened by the time he had spent in the smoke-filled public house. As for the "abominable" charge that had become the subject of so many rumours, the only direct accusation of indecency was made by George Rix. He swore that the curate had pushed him down in a hedgerow near Normanston Court and made an indecent suggestion to him. Rodgers, of course, denied anything of the sort had happened. He accused Rix of making it all up; the pupil-teacher had been very angry that day about not being allowed to go to the Yarmouth regatta and instead being forced to spend the entire day with a mob of schoolboys. Faced with two such contradictory accounts, the aged vicar concluded that the charges against his erstwhile curate - drunkenness and attempted indecent assault - were "not proven."

"Not proven" was not the same as "not guilty" and the residents of Lowestoft were free to believe as before. While the inquiry had been private, the allegation was now known by seemingly everyone and Mr. Rodgers' usefulness in Lowestoft was surely over. Moreover, he would have great difficulty in finding church employment elsewhere. No bishop would license him. He returned to London where he served as chaplain for Messrs. Copestake Moore & Co. – a mail order firm in Bow, London, dealing in "lace and sewed muslins, scotch and Manchester goods, cambrics & lawns, crapes, gossamers, velvets, stays, artificial flowers, millinery, baby linen, mantles, outfitting, shawl & haberdashery, umbrellas & parasols." Whilst it must have been some consolation to minister to the souls of those who were so fortunate to work at such an all-encompassing establishment, Mr. Rodgers could only agree with his erstwhile vicar, "Your only chance to return to society, or to your position in life, is boldly to confront your accusers, and let your innocence be publicly established."

* * *

The case of *Rodgers v Rix* was to be heard in the (then) splendid setting of the Suffolk County Hall in Ipswich. With a massive frontage of white brick and corner towers in a mock Tudor style, the Hall boasted two "commodious" courtrooms. On 3 August 1859, the Nisi Prius court was elbow-to-elbow with Lowestoft residents who made the forty-five mile journey. The plaintiff, the Rev. Mr. Rodgers, was seeking damages from the defendant

(Rix) for slander, i.e. for "certain words spoken" imputing the commission of an unnatural offence and an indecent assault.[85] Mr. Rodgers would not be required to prove the falsity of the slander. On the other side, Rix had pleaded justification. He was prepared to substantiate what he had said, in other words, that he spoke the truth. The case was heard before Mr. Justice William Wightman, a Scot "of excessive modesty and possessing an abundance of good sense."

Speaking for well over an hour, David Keane, the curate's young barrister, opened the case. "Never before,' he said, with perhaps pardonable exaggeration, had he taken on such a solemn burden. The jury would hear the truth of the events of that day and, Mr. Keane was confident, they would find their way to redeem a man's character that had been so foully aspersed. He called Charlie Trigg to the stand.

This was a slander action and the first duty for the plaintiff's counsel was to show that the defendant had indeed spoken the offending words. Trigg, a "pupil-teacher" just like George Rix, was asked if he remembered the events of the previous summer and he replied smartly, "Of course, I do, it was the year of the comet." Daneli's comet had caused a sensation during its pass over Britain in 1858. Charlie had also been on the outing, sitting in the same boat with George Rix. He remembered how George "got sick over the bows." But after returning to Mutford, Charlie had gone straight home and was not among those who tarried to drink and smoke at the *Wherry*. When the witness later heard people gossiping about the events that evening, he went to George Rix. Charlie swore that Rix, at first, resisted telling him. Eventually, Rix began talking about that night; on the return walk to Lowestoft, the curate had tried to indecently assault him. When they reached the hedgerows of Normanston Court, Rix recalled that Mr. Rodgers asked to sit down. And so they did. According to Charley Trigg, Rix told him:

> He threw himself on to me and began to pull me about. I pushed him off and saw that his trousers were undone. I took him by the coat and threw him into the middle of the road, and said I will knock you down with the wicket if you are not quiet. I then took hold of Mr. Rodgers' arm and led him down to the others, during which time he attempted it again; I could not pacify him only by threatening him with a wicket.

Rix told Trigg that he was furious with Rodgers and shoved him along the path. The curate staggered along – on his own - until they soon caught up with the others. When the boating party split up that night, Rix told Trigg that he went along to Whincup's place where they washed his trousers. Understandably, most of the newspapers considered Trigg's testimony, with the suggestion of an emission, to be "absolutely unfit for publication" in the otherwise extensive coverage of the trial. *The Suffolk Chronicle* provides the most explicit details.

According to Trigg's account, Rix told him that he had roughly pushed the curate away because he was "not like him." A few days later, Mr. Rodgers came to him (Rix) pleading, in tears, for his silence because "his bread" depended on it. Charlie Trigg told the court that he believed that Rix was ever bitter about being forced to miss the Yarmouth regatta for the schoolboy picnic. Prior to the Rev. Cunningham's private enquiry, Charlie remembered how Rix had boasted, "We'll give him a tucking up." [Rustic slang for a hanging.[86]]

The slander had, at last, been graphically quoted. What Rix claimed to have happened to him would certainly have met the legal definition of an "assault with the intent to commit sodomy." That crime was a misdemeanor punishable by a maximum two-year sentence.[87] The Rev. Edward Rodgers, the man so accused of such "unnatural conduct," dressed in his clerical suit of black, climbed the few stairs into the witness box. He was led through the desultory details of his education and clerical experience. Keane asked his witness if the story the defendant had told to Charley Trigg was true. Rodgers firmly stated that Rix's account was entirely false, "there is no truth in any of it whatsoever." Recounting the entire day of the outing, the curate denied being intoxicated. He had taken some ale at the staithe in Burgh and, an hour or two later, returning in the evening, he had some brandy at the *Wherry*. His difficulty in walking was due to his being "excessively tired" at the end of a long day in the heat and sun. He had been up early that morning to perform a wedding.

He then spent several hours on the Broads. The accident when Henderson fell into the river had been frightening and upsetting. And, finally, the thick smoke inside the pub made him extremely nauseous. He was not a strong man, given to spells of biliousness, and he walked home that night with great difficulty. Rix had taken his arm for a good deal of the way but nothing happened at any time. He remembered the entire evening. "I was not drunk," Rodgers swore. He shook hands with all four of his companions, George Rix included, and bid them good night.

It was several weeks later - at Adderton's shop - that Rodgers first learned that his name had been slandered in Lowestoft. He testified that it was only then that he confronted George Rix, whom he determined to be the source of the story. He did not beg Rix for forgiveness or silence but rather confronted the youth to accuse him of telling a malicious lie. Rodgers told the court that he and Rix had a serious dispute when he refused to allow the defendant to go to the Yarmouth regatta that day. In its heyday, the annual regatta was "a fair afloat where the voice of revelry resounds from every gliding tent."[88] Such was the regatta's reputation that Rodgers had determined it was "not a fit place for Rix to go." The curate had given Rix a choice – he could either go to the Regatta but lose his employment at the school or stay to help with the picnic. Rix had complied with the instructions but was sullen for most of the day. The curate ended his testimony by conceding that the slanders spread by Rix had cost him a curacy he had held for over five years in Lowestoft and forced him to take a much lesser position without any church duties.

The counsel for George Rix was William Metcalfe, a clergyman's son, by the way. After a few questions about what Rodgers had to drink that day, Metcalfe turned to the central question: the walk home. Rodgers had already testified that he had taken George Rix's arm. In fact, hadn't he asked specifically for George's assistance? He had. But when the others, who had gotten so far ahead, halted and looked back, they saw Rodgers and Rix coming out of that wooded stretch of the road, no longer arm-in-arm but walking apart. Metcalfe asked, "I want to know how you came to leave go of his arm?" Rodgers said he did not remember. Had there been a quarrel? "Absolutely not," Rodgers insisted. The witness did admit, however, that when he rejoined the others, still needing assistance, it was the arm of Moss not Rix that he took for the rest of the walk into Lowestoft.

The rest of the cross-examination dealt with Rodgers' actions after his visit to Adderton's shop. Rodgers had quickly sent word to Rix to come to his home but the curate denied Metcalfe's imputation that he had gone into hiding. He was ill, not being able to sleep for worry after hearing that people were accusing him of drunkenness and "other irregularities." At first, he thought the only charge he had to answer involved drink - which was nonetheless a very serious ecclesiastical offense. Rodgers simply wanted to know what Rix had been telling people. He denied begging Rix to tell the vicar that all this gossip was "a pack of nonsense." Nor did he recall Rix saying, "I am doing all I can to help you." Still, Rodgers conceded that he and his wife left Lowestoft for London only days later.

Mrs. Mary Jane Rodgers followed her husband's appearance; she testified that he returned that evening in a state of near collapse. He was exhausted but "quite sober." He slept for several hours and when he awoke she made him a brandy, with bicarbonate of soda and powdered ginger. It seemed to make him worse and the doctor was sent for. Her husband remained in bed for several days and when he was strong enough to re-emerge, she went out walking with him and he did not go "immediately" to see George Rix.

Dr. Meadows, who had come to see Rodgers the next morning, told the court that he found the curate to be both prostrated and excited. He prescribed an opium draught which he would not have done if he suspected alcohol was involved. The plaintiff had been his patient for several years and had been treated previously for nervousness, biliousness and sleeping problems. Questioned by Metcalfe, the doctor denied that Rodgers had done any crying when he attended him that morning, nor did his patient make any wild gestures or behave in anything like a hysterical manner.

Many of the newspaper accounts of the trial omitted any mention of the next witness, a maid-of-all-work named Charlotte Crouching. She was employed by the Rev. and Mrs. Rodgers and among her duties was brushing up the curate's clothes each morning. On the morning of 28 July 1858, she had tended to the clothes worn by Mr. Rodgers on the previous day. Mr. Deane, with discretion, inquired as to the condition of the curate's trousers. They were very dusty, the servant recalled, as if he had walked along a dusty road.

Q: "Were there any other marks?"

A: "No, sir, nothing else."

Why would George Rix have made up this vile story? Many residents of Lowestoft had formed that opinion. Thus, for Rev. Rodgers, it was important that he show a motive: George held a grudge against him for frustrating the lad's plans to attend the Yarmouth regatta. Frederick Wright was sworn to testify that, on the morning of the outing, an embittered Rix vowed, "I'll be buggered if I don't do for [Rodgers]." But the opposing counsel wondered why Wright had not mentioned this to anyone until this trial, more than a year later? Oh, but he had: Wright helpfully recalled that he and Charley Trigg had talked about it during their Sunday Bible class. The courtroom erupted in laughter which was gaveled down. Poor Wright also had to admit that he had recently spent time in jail for "mistreating an idiot."

A pair of Lowestoft woman gave evidence indicating that George Rix was quite open with his talk of vengeance against the curate. Margaret Jeffries and

Mary Ann Harling, in turn, swore to hearing the lad say how he was going "to do for Dicky Rodgers." But Miss Harling admitted that many people in Lowestoft had called the curate "Dicky Rodgers." At this time, "Dicky" generally referred to something inferior, or a person in bad health, being foggy, or queer (as in odd). "Dick" did not become associated with the penis until circa 1870.[89]

Several others who were on the outing swore to Mr. Rodgers' sobriety and good conduct on the day. And the vicar, Rev. Cunningham, testified that for more than five years, Rodgers had been an "assiduous and valuable" curate. When he first heard the horrid report, Cunningham had conducted a private investigation which, alas, ended only with a conclusion of "not proven." He had concluded at the time that, sadly, that he would have to ask for the curate's resignation. Metcalfe rose to ask the vicar how long he had known George Rix. It had been many years, certainly. Rix had been a pupil-teacher and in the Sunday-school program. What did the vicar think of him? "He has borne a very good character as long as I have known him." On that note, and certainly not the most helpful contribution, the case for the Rev. Mr. Rodgers rested.

In the opening statement for his young client, Metcalfe reminded the jury that this case was every bit as important to George Rix as it might be to the plaintiff. Only 18, George was already well-known in the town of Lowestoft. His father was a respected tradesman (a bricklayer) and the Rix family was numerous in the town and surrounding area. This young man stood accused of having made up the most horrible story to be told against any man, let alone a clergyman. And for what motive? Simply because he couldn't go to Yarmouth for one day? The defendant took the stand.

Once more, the jury heard the story of that long ago cheerful day on the Broads. George admitted drinking his share of beer and smoking a pipe at the *Wherry*. The day had ended pleasantly. But as they left to begin their walk back into town, he thought it was plain that Mr. Rodgers had "partaken too freely of drink." When the curate specifically asked for his help, George offered his arm. He remembered that Mr. Rodgers was hanging on to his arm in a "stupid" way and they fell far behind the others. Then, in the wooded path by Normanston Court, Rix said he agreed to sit down.

> We sat down on the bank. This was on the right hand side of the road going from Mutford to Lowestoft. It was a high bank with a hedge on the top. As I was sitting down he pushed his hands against my breast, and pushed me against the bank, and began to unbutton my trousers; his were unbuttoned. I caught hold of his collar and pushed him into the middle of the road. As he was doing this, he said, "Come, come, dear." I had three wickets in my hand, which Mr. Pratt asked me to take home. When I

pushed him into the road, he said, "What's the matter, George?" I told him it was a good job for him he did not go home with a broken head. I then went on to catch the others by myself. I reached them first, and Mr. Rodgers came up 3 or 4 minutes afterwards. He seemed to walk very irregularly. I told Mr. Barrett what "the plaintiff" had done to me, and I think in Mr. Whincup's hearing. I told Moss three or four nights after.

George acknowledged that he shook the curate's hand when the walkers separated. Rix then walked to Whincup's home, where he showed him the "mark" on his trousers. They washed it off.

Of course, the curate had denied under oath that anything like that had happened. He had also sworn that he never went to Rix asking for silence and forgiveness. But Rix next testified that, the Friday after the outing, Rodgers did come to him, to say his conduct at the outing was "weighing" on him. George told the curate that it was probably just too much drink but Rodgers insisted he wasn't drunk but "crazy" and his doctor would prove it. He asked George to tell no one. "Remember my wife and child,' he said, 'and my bread is in your hands." Rix did vow to keep the secret but he had already told any number of people. Thus, after Rodgers learned from Adderton that the story was known to various "dangerous" sorts, the curate called Rix to his home. George testified that Mrs. Rodgers took him upstairs where her husband was in bed. She was sent away. When George admitted that he had been unable to keep his promise, Rodgers began to cry and told him, "You are very cruel." Within a few days, Mr. and Mrs. Rodgers left for London.

When challenging someone's story – or "impeaching" a witness – barristers must look for inconsistencies or embellishments. Rix, of course, had appeared before the private enquiry conducted by the vicar of Lowestoft. It was not a court of law and whether there was any transcript of the proceedings is unknown. Still, Keane, the counsel for Mr. Rodgers, was quick to point out that Rix seemed to have added some sensational new details to his story. For the first time, Rix mentioned that the curate tried to unbutton *his* trousers. Nor had Rix previously claimed that Rodgers had said, "Come, come, dear." Rix could only say that he did not remember exactly what the conversation had been like that night but, as a result of the lawsuit, he had been forced to give a great deal of thought to the details. Things he had "forgotten" had become clearer. Keane suggested that Rix – having been sick in the boat earlier in the day – was intoxicated himself and that explained why they had fallen behind the others on the trail. And, if Rix had been drunk, how could he remember that night so clearly? But Rix insisted that while he may have been nauseous earlier in the day, he had never been sick. Keane asked whether it was well-known in Lowestoft that George had ill-will for Mr. Rodgers. The witness denied it. He denied ever calling the plaintiff "Dicky." He denied ever saying he planned to "do" for him, or "tuck him up." George even testified that he was never all that upset about missing his chance to go to joins the revels in Yarmouth. Keane continued with questions. Why didn't George tell his father immediately? The headmaster of the school, Mr. Pratt? Would it be proper for a man capable of such conduct to be around schoolboys? To all the questions, the witness answered, "I don't know." George also admitted that he never told Rev. Cunningham. In fact, George conceded that he had continued to attend services at St. Margaret's, conducted by Mr. Rodgers and had taken communion from his hands. The same hands that had supposedly pulled at his trousers? Could he explain that? George could not. It was nearly eight o'clock, most of ten hours had passed, when Justice Wightman adjourned for the night.

What was being called "The Diabolical Slander Case," resumed in the County Hall the next morning at nine. One after another, the counsel for George Rix called the three Lowestoft men who made up the rest of that small walking party returning from Mutford Bridge. Peter Barrett, the sexton at St. Margaret's, knew the curate very well and had never seen him the worse for drink. But he was certainly unsteady that night. Barrett recalled that when Rix caught up with them on the path, he seemed upset. Barrett asked what had happened and Rix said you must promise not to tell anyone. Rix claimed that the curate had pushed him to the ground and began trying to unbutton his trousers. The curate's "front flap" was already undone. But Rix said he managed to push him off and threatened him with a wicket from the day's cricket match. Under cross-examination, Barrett said he hadn't told the vicar because he was ashamed to speak of the whole thing, it was that disgusting. But not so disgusting that he continued to work with Mr. Rodgers at the church and attend his services.

Moss, the lighthouse keeper who took the curate's arm for the remaining portion of the walk, said there had been a good deal of drinking at the W*herry*. Did Mr. Rodgers have any gin, Moss was asked. He couldn't be sure but "there were three glasses of gin bought and they all disappeared." That night, he remembered that Rodgers, who was very wobbly on his feet, said, "Friend Moss, I can never undertake another day of this sort." Because he was walking with the curate, Moss said he did not hear Rix's tale until a day or so later.

Last to enter the box was Robert Whincup. It was he who quoted Rix as saying, with a laugh, "I guess he thought I was his wife." Whincup also supported the evidence that there was a substance on Rix's clothing. Whincup, rather graphically, said that at first he thought it was "fish slime." He helped Rix wash it off. Yet Whincup, too, did not deny that he had continued to attend services conducted by the Rev. Rodgers.

Before Metcalfe could begin his closing argument, Keane asked to call a final witness for the plaintiff: Mr. Pratt, the headmaster, was sworn and testified that George Rix did not have any wickets with him that night. Pratt had given the wickets to another lad to carry. Metcalfe, beginning his closing argument, shrugged off the entire question of the wickets. The wickets are wholly immaterial, he said, as was most of the evidence presented on Mr. Rodgers' behalf. Of far greater importance, Metcalfe asserted, was the fact that the Rev. Mr. Rodgers chose not to call as his witnesses the only other people on earth who had actual knowledge of the "transactions" of that evening - Messrs. Barrett, Moss and Whincup. Instead, all three men, adults and respected in the town of Lowestoft, came forward to entirely corroborate George Rix's statement. Can anyone really believe that George Rix would have made up such an unspeakable story simply because he did not get to go to Yarmouth? Mr. Rodgers believed the regatta was not a fit place for George Rix yet the very same clergyman – responsible for an outing for parish schoolchildren – spent hours drinking, smoking and idling at various inns. It's a wonder just one child fell into the water. The truth of George Rix's account, Metcalfe averred, can be seen in the actions of the Rev. Rodgers. When the plaintiff learned that the secret was out - as secrets will always get out - what did he do? He "skulked away." The curate quickly realized that "his name stank in the town." Even his own vicar had believed him guilty. The Rev. Rodgers had left Lowestoft once and he should have stayed away. Metcalfe asked the jury to show by their verdict that they do not wish to restore him to society but, rather, "expel him as they would any other pest."

Replying to his "learned friend," Mr. Keane said the reason he had not called the others was simply because he did not believe them. Why had these so-called respectable men not immediately reported such disgraceful behaviour to their much-loved vicar? Particularly Barrett, the very sexton of the church, a man entrusted to be the "caretaker" of St. Margaret's. Yet, Barrett testified that he allowed a man he believed guilty of an abominable crime, to hold services, perform marriages, bury the dead and enjoy the society of the parishioners of Lowestoft for more than six months. Barrett testified that he had been "too disgusted" to go to Rev. Cunningham. Keane believed the jury would find that - as he had - unbelievable. The truth was that Mr. Rodgers was not well when he set off home that night. Bilious and over-excited, exhausted by the long day, shaken by the near drowning of a schoolboy, sickened by two hours in a smoke-filled pub where he drank but one brandy, it was a struggle for him simply to walk. George Rix gave him an arm; he had to physically hold the man up at times. They naturally fell behind. But nothing had happened in the wooded lane. Who knew why George wanted to "do for Dicky Rogers?" Several witnesses heard him say as much. To miss the regatta was, no doubt, a disappointment. George, no more than eighteen, made up a story, perhaps as a joke, and then could not call it back. All the curate wanted now was justice and the restoration of his long-standing good name in Lowestoft. Keane felt great confidence in leaving the case in their hands.

What was the jury to do? They had heard two contradictory accounts of the events of the previous July. But, really, don't all trials come down to choosing between conflicting versions of "facts?" It had been a long two days for everyone, Justice Wightman agreed, but the attention paid was deserved because it involved a question of the greatest importance. A man's reputation was at stake. The allegation of drunkenness against Mr. Rodgers was a minor matter. Wightman instructed the jurymen on the law of slander: to impute to someone the commission of a criminal offense (i.e. an unnatural crime) was actionable. It was even more so when such a claim would be "injurious" to the plaintiff in his (or her) profession. Certainly that was true for a clergyman such as Rodgers. That said, the jury would have to decide whether they believed George Rix's tale or not. His counsel had argued that there was no credible reason for a young man who had known and worked with the plaintiff for several years to suddenly make up such a filthy story. The other side, however, offered evidence that George Rix, so upset that he could not attend the Yarmouth regatta, had vowed to "do" for Mr. Rodgers. The jury must choose which side was worthy of a verdict. Taking with them the exchange of letters between the curate and his vicar, the jury left the room.

The Rev. Mr. Rodgers had requested a "special jury." Either party in an action, most often the plaintiff, rather than take the next twelve men on the list, could request that the jury be made up of men who are "legally entitled to be called an esquire, or shall be a person of higher degree, or shall be a banker or merchant." They were presumed to be "persons of superior intelligence." The consideration was one of cost as the special jurors were paid a guinea a day[90], added to the other costs of the bringing the suit. The "special" jurors returned to the courtroom after just less than one hour to announce that they had found for the plaintiff, Rev. Rodgers. The news accounts do not record any public demonstrations of approval or disapproval with the jury's finding. Mr. Keane said his client was, of course, delighted with the verdict and had no wish to seek significant damages from the defendant. What resources would a bricklayer's son have had to pay them anyway? If, for the record, Justice Wightman would state from the bench that the Rev. Mr. Rodgers' character had been cleared, then the curate would agree to accept nugatory damages - the sum of 40 shillings. Wightman demurred from making any formal statement, saying only Mr. Rodgers had come to court to deny "the offense imputed to him" and a jury had found in his favour. Damages of forty shillings were so ordered.

The Rev. Edward Rodgers, erstwhile curate of Lowestoft, left the courtroom and East Anglia with his name and character ostensibly cleared, but he would not find it easy to secure suitable employment in the church. He returned to being chaplain to the workers at a London warehouse. In 1862, he received an appointment to be a curate at

Christ Church in New Radford, a section of Nottingham. He was there for three years; his wife ran the Sunday School and when they left, they received the typical gifts, an inkstand, a chair etc., all "gratifying proof of the good will [they] engendered in the parish." Rodgers spent the rest of his life, 35 years, as vicar of St. Luke's, a poor and populous parish in Nottingham. Interestingly, Rodgers' later detailed entries in *Crockford's Clerical Directory* either omit or make only the briefest mention of his six years in Lowestoft. They were apparently "over-exciting" times best forgotten.

5. THE IRREPROACHABLE MR. KARR

The Rev. John Seton Karr, Vicar of Berkeley

St. Mary's, Berkeley (2016)

Two miles inland from the Severn, in a delightful vale, stands the ancient village of Berkeley. It was never a great nor populous settlement but ever famous for Berkeley Castle, "one of the finest and most perfect feudal fortresses in this kingdom."[91] There has been a castle in Berkeley for almost a millennium. Infamously, Edward II, while prisoner at the castle, was murdered there in 1327. The Berkeleys were somehow able to explain away their involvement in the regicide. For centuries since, as bankers and landowners, with holdings from Berkeley House in London to Gloucestershire, the family flourished. But by the time of Victoria's reign, the Berkeleys as a noble family had become notorious. The story is a fascinating one which repays attention, however, for the purposes of this account, a brief summary shall suffice.

The fifth Earl of Berkeley married a butcher's daughter named Mary Cole; alas, he claimed to have married her twice. The authenticity of the first marriage was rejected by the House of Lords. Thus, the first seven of their thirteen children were illegitimate. In consolation, the first born son was given a new title, the first Earl Fitzhardinge. The sixth son, being the first legitimate male, should have been the new Earl of Berkeley, but either due to intimidation or indifference, he took a pass. He chose not to usurp his eldest brother, who was clearly his mother's darling. Thus, Fitzhardinge had the castle but not the coronet. A "vulgar, narrow-minded man," he resided in Berkeley through the years with a succession of mistresses.[92].

Just a short walk beyond the irregular walls of the Berkeley fortress lies St. Mary's Church. As with the castle, the church - of "almost cathedral-like proportions" - is much larger than the small village would seem to require. Despite their irregular domestic arrangements, the Berkeleys remained patrons of the parish, presenting the living to a series of vicars. With their louche patron and protector behind the castle walls, these clergymen have been rather harshly described as the "obsequious vicars of Berkeley."[93]

The latest of these clerics and the subject of our story was the Rev. John Seton-Karr who arrived in Berkeley, just 25 years old, in 1839. His father was John Seton, a civil servant in Bengal who added the (sometimes-hyphenated) Karr upon his return to Britain and settled on a small estate in Scotland. John, the eldest son, went to Cambridge but owing to a scandal with a married woman[94], he left for Oxford, taking his degree and ordination in successive years. Arriving as the new vicar of Berkeley, he created an instant impression.

> [He was] an exquisite of the first water — a clerical dandy entirely irreproachable. He was a young fellow of the "oiled and curled Assyrian bull" species.[95] Well built, with a handsome face, raven black hair and the neatest of curled whiskers, faultless in attire, a capital reader and a good preacher (in an academical way), Mr. Karr considerably fluttered the country-side at his coming. Many gentle bosoms were excited by the presence of such a paragon in the pulpit.[96]

Indeed. In 1844, with the vicar's thirtieth birthday approaching, several ladies of the parish felt the need to honour him by knitting a carpet displaying his coat-of-arms. Taking the lead in this charming project was Mrs. Elizabeth Gaisford. Her husband, William, was a local solicitor who worked closely with Rev. Karr, both in collecting the church tithes and as clerk to the local magistrates, where, ex-officio, the vicar was pleased to serve. Mrs. Gaisford went to Bath where she personally selected the wool for the new carpet and reserved for herself the handiwork in the center. With mullets, stags, eagles and separate mottoes for the Setons and Karrs[97], it must have been quite the project. Certainly it required numerous visits to the vicarage for measurements and consults. Fortunately, the vicarage in Mary Brook was only a few steps away from the Gaisford home in the Market Square.

William and Elizabeth Gaisford were married in 1835 and had four sons. As a well-respected solicitor, William wore many hats in Berkeley and in Gloucestershire affairs, in general. He traveled the county frequently. His wife did not lack for company as living with them was Mrs. Elizabeth Amyas, a clergyman's widow, who had raised Mrs. Gaisford from childhood. William was a year older than his wife; Elizabeth was, perhaps, three years older than the vicar. Of her personal appearance, the evidence is scanty. She was described as taller than average, perhaps close to 5-foot-6. Her most remarked upon attribute was a set of fine, if regrettably prominent, teeth.

Apparently, the professional and personal relations between the Rev. Mr. Seton-Karr and the Gaisfords were unremarkable until the year 1846. It was Mrs. Amyas who first took notice of what she thought were disturbing liberties being taken by the handsome young clergyman and Mrs. Gaisford. The Rev. Mr. Karr was a true "sporting parson," riding with the raffish hunting set that gathered at Berkeley Castle. But he also shared his time and interests with his parishioners. In June 1846, he organized a "water party," including the Gaisfords, Mrs. Amyas, and a few of the "better" people. A keen angler, the vicar - and his guests - were off to Portishead on the Severn, "a place of some celebrity as a fishing ground." Mrs. Amyas took notice of how the vicar artfully arranged the two boats so as to push off with Mrs. Gaisford beside him, while her husband was consigned to the other craft. When the boats returned, the watchful lady was quite aghast to see where the clergyman placed his hand to assist Elizabeth, a married woman, onto the dock!

Stewing on that little incident, Mrs. Amyas was especially vigilant at the next little "do" in Berkeley. Archery was then the thing among the country gentry. It was an "elegant and healthy amusement" that could be enjoyed by both sexes. In the field behind the Gaisford home, targets were set up and contests held. Again, it wasn't exactly the "castle set," but the vicar deigned to join them. But Mr. Karr and Elizabeth were now being observed. Look at how they scampered off together, laughing, to check the targets after each round. As they stooped to pick up the errant arrows, their hands would occasionally touch, without recoil.

William seemed oblivious to this questionable conduct on the part of his wife but Mrs. Amyas was in something near shock. Worse was to come at the refreshment table following the archery. It was a time for gaiety and banter and the vicar was seated (where else but) next to Elizabeth. The older woman would swear to seeing Mrs. Gaisford's hand resting on the clergyman's thigh. Mrs. Amyas, now beside herself entirely, drew William aside; she wondered how he was not seeing this brazen conduct. She suggested the crafty strategy of casually picking up a newspaper, dropping it near the table, then bending down to pick it up and seeing for himself. Which he did, perhaps clumsily, and what did he see? The poor man later claimed to have observed his wife's hand resting on the clergyman's arm, while the gentleman's casually outstretched leg just so happened to be inappropriately nestled beneath Mrs. Gaisford's petticoat.

There was no immediate scene. The afternoon ended civilly. But William was now also on the scent. He and Mrs. Amyas spoke sharply with Elizabeth; her conduct with Mr. Karr was unacceptable and would have to end. The man was dangerous. The Cambridge incident was raised. His castle morals were not those of decent people. A previously accepted invitation for another water-party on the Severn was cancelled. The vicar actually called upon the Gaisfords out of concern that someone might have been ill in the house.

Elizabeth told him what had happened and how William's mind had been "poisoned" against him.

The following Sunday, 28 June, the Gaisford family was in their customary pew at St. Mary's. Even there, in church, there was unease. Ever-alert, Mrs. Amyas thought she detected Elizabeth seating the children in a way that reserved for herself the space with the most direct eye contact with the vicar. Mr. Karr, of course, who seemed to "float upward with flowing sleeves like wings," climbed the stairs to his lofty pulpit whence he surveyed the entire congregation, having sprung open the cover of his splendid gold watch and set it upon a cushion. Elizabeth looked up adoringly.

William had begun to keep daily notes, as solicitors are wont to do. His anger grew each day. On 30 June, he went to the vicarage to confront the Rev. Karr who was at his breakfast. William declined to join him. He had come to demand that Mr. Karr leave Elizabeth alone. All improper familiarities between them must cease. Karr demanded an explanation and Gaisford recounted everything, stressing the disgraceful scene beneath the tea table. As a man who travels in society, Karr joked that given the state of feminine fashion and the size of the small table, it would be almost impossible for a gentleman not to place his foot under some lady's garment. And Mrs. Gaisford was not resting her hand on him, the vicar insisted. It seems that Karr had been chaffing Gaisford on his abysmal archery talents, and while it amused others at the table, it plainly annoyed her husband and she had gently nudged the vicar with her hand, urging him to let the matter drop. These smooth answers would not work. William would not listen. He was a simple country solicitor and a husband and father. He appealed to Karr, "Pray, do not ruin my peace." Again, acting the part of a good solicitor, Gaisford had prepared a document asking that Karr agree to cease all contact with his wife except "such as cannot be avoided in mixed society." The vicar said the demand was insulting, to himself and to Mrs. Gaisford. He would sign the document only if it also included his oath that nothing improper had occurred between them. Then, solely in the interest of village comity, Mr. Karr signed.

Comity prevailed in Berkeley, at least between the vicarage and the Gaisfords. In fact, in late November, Rev. Karr gave a dinner for his churchwardens and other key members of the parish laity, their wives included. Of course, Mr. Gaisford would be invited. The evening came off most pleasantly. So much so that, once at home, William Gaisford allowed himself to briefly think that the danger had passed. Early in 1847, he boldly invited Mr. Karr to a "quadrille." Perhaps, he had no other choice. Though Berkeley had as many as 4000 residents (mostly farmers, dairymen and lower tradesmen), the actual number who moved in the "mixed society" of the Gaisfords was quite small. Entertaining was expected and not to have invited Mr. Karr, without some very good reason, would have excited comment. The quadrille was a safe dance; the gentlemen move from female partner to partner "like a bee from flower to flower."[98]

And, to be sure, dear Mrs. Amyas would have the vicar under her eye at all times.

Overall, 1847 seemed to be a year of quietus in the building Berkeley scandal. The year was dominated by politics and another row in the Berkeley family. At the castle, Earl Fitzhardinge had long controlled the two local seats in Parliament; one of them had been held by his younger (legitimate) brother, Grantley Berkeley. But the Earl and Grantley had fallen out and Fitzhardinge recruited a nephew to contest the seat. It was a bitter and hugely costly election. William Gaisford, as a "political agent," was employed by the nephew and escorted him throughout the West Gloucestershire constituency. At one point, luckless William was set upon by roughs loyal to Grantley but he managed to escape with nothing more than a crushed hat. William's man was beaten at the polls but the point of interest here is that all this electioneering kept him away from home and quite distracted for much of 1847. William was not away all the time; late in the year, Elizabeth was expecting a child. It is important to state that never, in the ensuing deluge of litigation, was it ever suggested that the Rev. Karr was the father of this coming baby.

On a frosty night in late January 1848, the Rev. Karr had invited the usual people to the vicarage for a waltz. Once condemned as an "indecent foreign dance," the waltz had been legitimised as it was the favourite dance of the Queen and Prince Albert. Mr. Karr kept no piano and he had asked William to borrow his which had been arranged.

William would rather not have gone to the dance but, again for reasons of "comity," he agreed to attend. He and Elizabeth brought along their eldest son, 10 year old Charles. Several of the other guests would recall that William moped about for much of the evening and seemed most unhappy. When Mr. Karr approached to ask for permission to dance with Elizabeth, William refused. Whether it was out of concern for her "condition" or it was intended to be an insult to the vicar was left to the judgement of those who observed the brief exchange. The Gaisfords soon departed; it was said that young Charley, who helped himself freely to the sweets, was the only one who had a good time.

A few weeks later, Elizabeth Gaisford lost her baby. To recuperate, she went to stay with a friend in Bath, remaining there until late April. When she returned to Berkeley, the Rev. Mr. Karr called several times, also sending notes, to ask for her health. Elizabeth was well enough to attend Easter services at St. Mary's and received communion from the vicar. A day or so later, Karr left for London, to handle some personal business and to preside at his brother's wedding. News of the vicar's departure was generally known in Berkeley. Fewer people knew that Mrs. Gaisford had also left for the capital.

Everything that has been recounted to this point would have been broadly accepted as a fair narrative of the rising tensions between Messrs. Karr and Gaisford. To be sure, the vicar would have scoffed at how Gaisford had made so much from so little. On his part, the solicitor would argue that it was all prelude to the eventual destruction of his marital home. From 27 April 1848, however, two dramatically contradictory stories were told.

Mrs. Gaisford's trip to London was not taken in stealth. An old friend, Mrs. Phelps lived in Oxford Square, north of Hyde Park. She had been urging Elizabeth to visit for some time. Her strength restored after losing the baby, Elizabeth was at last capable of making that 127 mile journey. She had also promised William that, while in London, she would pay a call on some of his Gaisford relations, five (apparently) unmarried sisters who lived together in Hackney.

As for the Rev. Karr, he had checked in to Fladong's Hotel, a rather dated establishment, on the decline since the Regency but once popular with naval officers. It was located on Oxford Street at Cavendish Square; the vicar had taken Room 32, with a bedroom and a sitting room. On Thursday, 27 April, at the church of All Souls', Langham Place, Karr performed the marriage service for his younger brother, George. The groom was employed in the India Office and his bride was heiress to a timber fortune and lived in Portland Place. It was an excellent marriage, mentioned in all the right society papers, but there was no extended coverage of the event, and thus no guest list can be found. We can have no way of knowing if, as was later alleged, Elizabeth had been seen at the church.

The next day, a dreary wet Friday, Mrs. Gaisford – though she did not give her name – arrived at

Fladong's, asking to see the Rev. Mr. Karr. He was expecting her, she assured the man at the desk. A chambermaid was sent up and returned with the clergyman's instruction that the visitor be shown up to the sitting room. It is interesting to note that, at first, Karr flatly denied any such rendezvous at Fladong's had ever taken place. But later, confronted with eyewitness testimony, he would concede she had been there but no more than that. Her visit was quite brief. She was seen to leave the hotel, going across the street to a shop where she waited for a few minutes. A gentleman – very clearly identified as the vicar of Berkeley – then arrived in a rather bright orange cab. He helped Mrs. Gaisford into the vehicle, climbed in himself, and the driver trotted off in an easterly direction down Oxford Street. It was just about eleven o'clock in the morning. Early that afternoon, perhaps a little later than she planned, Mrs. Gaisford paid her call on the Misses Gaisford at their home in Sutton Place, Hackney. Consequently, anywhere from two to three hours were unaccounted for. The mystery of those missing hours gave rise to sensational, salacious and expensive litigation in both civil and ecclesiastical courts. One side or the other was guilty of outrageous perjury and conspiracy. The war was on.

While Elizabeth was in London, Mrs. Amyas apparently used this absence as an opportunity to go through her papers. She discovered several notes from the Rev. Karr to Elizabeth, mostly inquiring as to her health. The wording was solicitous and affectionate but trespassed on emotions that a gentleman should not express to another man's wife. Of course, Mrs. Amyas showed the letters to William who marched off again to the vicarage only to be horrorstruck to learn that the wicked man was also away in London. Gaisford maintained that under no circumstances would he have allowed his wife to go to London alone while the unscrupulous Mr. Karr was at large in the city. The solicitor was on the next train and retrieved his wife from Oxford Square. There were more scenes in the Gaisford home as would be expected. Mrs. Amyas called upon Karr, who had returned to the vicarage, to ask if he had received any letters or notes from Elizabeth. She reported back that the insufferable man just laughed and said, "I toss all my correspondence in the grate." William was now functionally unhinged with jealousy and suspicion. Elizabeth was being kept a virtual prisoner; her communication with even the rather limited "outside world" in Berkeley was strictly monitored. Gaisford forbade his wife to see the children and on 9 June, she left Berkeley forever.

William was now obsessed with bringing ruin upon the vicar. He pestered Karr with threats to expose his immorality, vowing to discover exactly what had happened in London. Even "the Castle" wouldn't be able to save him from disgrace. Incredibly, Gaisford was still serving as the tithe agent for St. Mary's church. Karr demanded his resignation; then, he simply sacked the man.

There was no (relatively) affordable path to divorce for the middle classes in Britain until 1857. But there were other means for Gaisford to exact his revenge. The Right Rev. Bishop of Gloucester was James Monk. Nearly sixty, Monk was to be harassed almost into his grave by the Gaisford-Karr scandal. Berkeley was in his diocese and he certainly had no use for the rollicking noble Berkeleys as a family. The Bishop had repeatedly declined invitations to visit the castle; to acknowledge and sanction the presence of "Mrs. Barker" was impossible. In the House of Lords, Monk and Fitzhardinge had angrily clashed in a debate over – of all things - a bill for the suppression of brothels. The reader will know on which side the Bishop was to be counted. William Gaisford beat a steady path from Berkeley to the Bishop's Palace demanding an official church enquiry into the conduct of the Rev. Mr. Karr. Of course, the Bishop knew that Karr was a castle intimate which was a mark against the man. Still, sneaking a cuddle in a boat or a hand-hold 'neath the cloth, although infuriating to a decent husband, hardly rose to the level of ecclesiastical depravity worthy of starting up the ancient and quite expensive process of disciplining a clergyman. Then again, if sustainable proof of adultery could be acquired, the bishop's secretary would be most interested to have a look.

Gaisford's obsessional search for the "smoking gun" led him to Thomas Ruther, a Berkeley labourer recently fired as a sometime gardener at the vicarage. Ruther came to William with the shocking bit of information that the Rev. Karr's true mistress was Sarah Barrow, the vicarage housekeeper. This "very pretty young woman" had been in the vicar's employment for some time and their unseemly familiarity was long the topic of village gossip. In May 1849, she married a local policeman. But, according to Ruther, within days of her wedding, Sarah realized she was pregnant and the father could only have been Mr. Karr. In despair, she went to her lover, the vicar. So went Ruther's tale, that Mr. Karr chose him - (his gardener?) to quietly call upon the local doctor for a powder "to destroy young'uns."

In fairness to Mr. Karr and the young lady, it was the common consent locally that Thomas Ruther held the title of "the greatest liar in Gloucestershire." After he had been sacked, another of the vicarage maidservants heard Ruther vow his revenge: "He [Mr. Karr] will find that I am a rum one. I'll just go across to that little fellow Gaisford and he will be glad to get hold of this to take that black rag of a gown off his back." Mr. Karr easily won a slander action against the slippery Ruther.[99]

There was certainly no ecclesiastical rule against having a pretty housekeeper[100] but the Ruther allegations spoke to the vicious range of gossip in Berkeley that surrounded the once "irreproachable" Mr. Karr. A tipping point had, at last, been reached. The Bishop authorised an enquiry; the Rev. Karr was notified and allowed to attend but he could not question any of the witnesses who appeared before a panel of local clergymen. What these men heard – including new evidence about the day at Fladong's hotel - was enough to convince Bishop Monk to refer the case to the Court of Arches in London, the highest disciplinary tribunal in the Church of England. In the meantime, effective on Sunday, 16 December 1849, the Rev. John Seton Karr was "inhibited from performing his sacred duties." Several parishioners, including Earl Fitzhardinge, of course, signed a protest letter to the Bishop, stating their "entire disbelief" in the claims against the vicar. The Bishop was unmoved; the preliminary investigation had left a clear impression of [Karr's] guilt.

> His ministrations must be worse than useless while such foul imputations were pending against him, I deemed it my imperative duty to follow the course which the law had prescribed. Nothing can be more offensive to the religious feelings of the people than that the Word of God should be pronounced, and the holy sacrament administered, by one who is at the same moment himself charged with scandalous immorality.

The *Bristol Times*, longtime critics of the Berkeley interest, remarked: "The pastor appears to have been hardly less fortunate than the peers of Berkeley in escaping the scandals of the world."

The Bishop's case (officially known as *Madan v. Karr*) was formally brought to the Court of Arches in London on 21 February 1850, to meet the requirement that any action must begin within two years of the alleged wrong-doing. Gaisford, relying on his well-paid investigator in London, a certain Mr. Jettings, claimed to have evidence that on 28 April 1848, Mr. Karr had taken Mrs. Gaisford by cab to a house of ill-fame in Hackney. The same new evidence would form the crux of Gaisford's separate civil action for "criminal-conversation" against the vicar, to be known as *Gaisford v. Karr.* But before either of those two actions could be heard, the Rev. Karr had also gone into court in Gloucester charging the gossipy Thomas Ruther with slander. The vicar won his case but the Gloucester jurymen made their point by awarding him naught but a single shilling for his troubles. It was a three-ring legal circus.

In the Court of Arches, investigators for the church, known as proctors, prepared the case. For weeks, the proctors worked out of the *Bell,* an old coaching hotel in Gloucester, interviewing witnesses, almost all of them recruited by William Gaisford, who was reimbursed for his efforts. Many of the witnesses from London were brought by train out to Berkeley, escorted into town and asked to surreptitiously identify the embattled vicar. So frequently was Mr. Karr followed about by skulking observers that, at least once, he lost his temper, furiously waving his stick. Similarly, Mrs. Gaisford was pursued about Bath to the point that she left for Boulogne. But the proctors crossed the Channel as well, witnesses in tow, while the expenses continued to mount. The Bishop would pay, of course. It was said that many people were "living off" the Berkeley scandal and none more so than William Gaisford himself.

Whatever money Gaisford was collecting from the proctors would be small change compared with the £10,000 in damages he now sought from the Rev. Mr. Karr in a separate suit for "criminal conversation" that was filed in August 1850. Crim. Con., as it was known, allowed a husband (but never a wife) to recover damages from an adulterer for the "dishonour of his bed, the alienation of his wife's affection and the destruction of his domestic comfort and the resulting mental anguish." Thus, Mr. Karr was a defendant in two separate actions – one ecclesiastical, targeting his profession as a clergyman, the second a civil tort action, branding him an adulterer and mulcting from him enormous financial damages.

The Arches case would be heard first – the case of *Madan v. Karr* began on 7 February 1851. The Arches court was located in a "lazy old nook" down an alley near St. Paul's. Within, everything was done with religious solemnity. Bells and prayers began each day. On 7 February 1851, the 73-year old dean of the Arches Court, Sir Herbert Jenner Fust, had to be carried up to his elevated bench[101]. Many church disciplinarians believed that Fust was predisposed to leniency and he was frequently attacked in the leader columns. The formal charge against the vicar of Berkeley was that he engaged in "profane cursing and swearing, lewd and indecent conduct and conversation; permitting and encouraging lewd and indecent conduct in his household, having been repeatedly guilty of adultery, fornication or incontinence, and of acts of drunkenness, and having by his excesses and irregularities, and conduct and demeanor, unbecoming a clergyman, brought great scandal upon the church."

The household evidence – basically the matter of Karr's alleged misconduct with Sarah Barrow, the housekeeper – was heard first. The Arches case, however, would always rise or fall on the more serious claim that Mr. Karr had committed adultery with Mrs. Elizabeth Gaisford. Time was wasted on the tittle-tattle of archery games, quadrilles, satin shoes and water parties. Dr. Harding, Karr's counsel, dismissed all that under the heading of "what is vulgarly called flirting." Eventually, the inquiry would get around to the events in London. Witnesses were sworn to say that a woman they later identified as Mrs. Gaisford had been at All Souls' Church for the wedding on 27 April 1848 and that she spoke to the Rev. Mr. Karr. The purpose of that conversation, according to the promoters (i.e. the Church forces), was to arrange the assignation for the following day. That next morning, Mrs. Gaisford left Oxford Square shortly before ten. Despite the wet weather, she declined a servant's offer to get her a cab. She would have had to tell the servant her destination. The housemaid also remembered - with curiously precise detail - what Mrs. Gaisford wore that day: a black velvet dress, white straw bonnet fastened with a colored ribbon, and a white lace veil. She wore a large Paisley shawl of different colors, fastened with a large cameo brooch. A woman wearing such clothing arrived at Fladong's Hotel about 10:30. The chambermaid who showed her up to Mr. Karr's sitting room confirmed it was her. The woman stayed no more than ten minutes. Brooks, a painter working on the Old Cavendish Street side of the hotel saw a woman, "with fine large teeth" leaving the hotel, alone, and taking brief shelter at a shop across the street. Minutes later, an orange "cabriolet" arrived. A gentleman in clerical attire, a man that Brooks had later identified as Mr. Karr, left in the cab with the toothsome woman, all heading east on Oxford Street.

The most important witnesses were the cabmen – there were two of them, because, it was alleged, that Mr. Karr had craftily changed cabs to throw off any possible followers. George Collins, the first cabman, took the man and woman from Henrietta Street, across from Fladong's, down Oxford Street, into Holborn and into the City, leaving them in the Poultry. When they got out of his cab, Collins watched them cross over the road and get into another cab in front of the European Coffee House. That cab rolled off, turning into Bishopsgate, and out of his sight. Collins had since formally identified both Mr. Karr and Mrs. Gaisford as his passengers on that day. The second cab mentioned was driven by George Salmon. He recalled the man and woman - whom he had also been able to identify - got into his cab at about 11:30. The instructions were vague: he was told to head for the Hackney Road. Once there, the gentleman - seeing a pub, The Roebuck - suggested they stop. Salmon testified that the man asked if he could buy him some beer. Inside the public house, the man - in a low voice - asked Salmon if he knew of any "respectable" houses in that part of London where a gentleman could bring a lady. A good cabman must have "the knowledge" and the helpful Salmon suggested a house in Weymouth Terrace. The cabman swore that he drove the couple to that location and received his 2s fare (and a free pint.) Salmon admitted that he normally kept a very detailed logbook of his fares but the volume for that period had unfortunately been misplaced.

Before the Arches court, Mr. Karr flatly denied that he met or saw Mrs. Gaisford at any time while in London that April. He presented an alibi for the hours when he was supposedly gallivanting off to Hackney for a leg-over in a "respectable" brothel. The vital testimony of the cabmen was ridiculed as utterly false. Collins, for instance, was a longtime friend of Jettings, the man employed by Gaisford to "get up" the case. Salmon, meanwhile, was motivated entirely by his lust for a reward. They were unbelievable witnesses, the defense team argued.

Testimony was heard over eight separate days, with the Dean of Arches adjourning the proceedings on March 15th to consider his verdict. Before departing, however, Fust indicated his concern that several of the witnesses for the promoters (the anti-Karr forces) had clearly been "tutored in the most flagrant manner," leaving him to conclude that "everything here is not as represented." The Dean's ruling would not come until after the civil action had been completed. Thus, the Rev. Mr. Karr had to scramble from the as-yet undecided ecclesiastical court in London to a civil court in Gloucester to answer the crim-con charge, proceedings which opened on 5 April 1851.

The Arches case, as noted, had covered all the gossip and rumours accumulated over many years in Berkeley. Archery parties, pianoforte exchanges and note-passing may bring the vapors to old Mrs. Amyas but for Mr. Gaisford to get his revenge (and £10,000) he would need much more. The crim-con case concentrated solely on that single day in April 1848. The evidence of the hotel staff, cabmen, etc., was strikingly similar - with one quite interesting exception. In the Arches Court, Karr denied any contact with Mrs. Gaisford in London. However, in the crim-con case, he admitted that she had, in fact, come to Fladong's hotel. He met with her there innocently and very briefly, and then put her in a cab and had no more to do with her.

In Gloucester's Shire Hall, the large polygonal courtroom held well over 200 people and it was filled with churchmen and, it seemed, most of the residents of Berkeley. Mr. Gaisford's lawyer presented a familiar series of witnesses who had been at Fladong's hotel that day in 1848: the desk clerk, the chambermaid, and the painters. The woman matching the description of Mrs. Gaisford came in about 10:30 that morning asking to see the Rev. Karr. She spent perhaps ten minutes in the vicar's sitting room. A "stunning, fine lady" with her remarkable teeth, she was seen leaving the hotel at about 11 o'clock. Moments later, in Henrietta Street, an orange-coloured cabriolet arrived; a gentleman in clerical attire stepped out and helped the woman into the vehicle.

Nearly three years had lapsed since the day in question, but the all-important memories of the cabmen were fresh (or had been freshened or wettened, or both.) George Collins, the first of the two drivers, enhanced his testimony for the court. Leaving the hotel, whilst in Oxford Street, he was asked to stop. The passengers went into the Pantheon, a fancy goods shop, returning with a new pair of leather gloves for the lady. As he drove down High Holborn, Collins heard what he thought was a knock and opening the roof-top door to inquire, he was shocked to observe "the lady with one leg on one side of the seat and the other leg on the other side, and the gentleman between the lady's legs." He admitted not seeing what exactly the gentleman "was about" or the state of the ladies undergarments. He had closed the trap door quickly - as any gentleman would. He dropped both passengers in Poultry, near the Mansion House. He watched them cross the street and get in another cab. He later found mud and dirt, as if from boots, on the seats of his cab. The very next day, according to Collins, he was waiting at his usual stand in Oxford Street, when the clergyman found him again and gave him 2s and suggested, "You need not say where you drove a lady and gentleman yesterday."

As for cabman No. 2, Salmon was certain that he could identify the man and woman he picked up near Mansion House. He remembered the lady well, because she had "white and large teeth" and he was struck by her dress, which he thought was "rather gay" for the time of day. A jury of twelve men of Gloucester, who may never have been to London, heard the details of the route out to Hackney, including the stops at the Roebuck and, finally, the "house of ill-fame" nearby. Salmon recalled telling his good wife that evening, over an 'umble dinner, "I thought it was a runaway wedding." The cabman freely admitted that he had come forward after an advertised award. He was paid to go to Berkeley to identify Rev. Karr, which - after one mistake - he did. He was then taken all the way to Boulogne where he identified Mrs. Gaisford.

According to Salmon's recollection, he had left the man and woman in Weymouth Street at about 12:30. There was a ninety minute gap in Mrs. Gaisford's movements, allegedly, as Miss Julia Gaisford testified that Elizabeth did not arrive at her home in Hackney until about two that afternoon. They had expected her earlier and did not wait lunch for her. They were finishing their midday repast when their country relation tardily arrived. Miss Julia also noted that Mrs. Gaisford appeared wearing a new pair of white leather gloves. The last witness was the housemaid at Oxford Terrace where Mrs. Gaisford had been staying. The young woman testified that there was nothing unusual about their guest when she returned home that April night except that she did not put her "underclothing" in the basket to be washed as usual.

Henry Keating QC was the Rev. Karr's legal voice in the crim-con trial. Let us not forget that the legal costs for Rev. Karr, fighting to preserve his good name and career, were also formidable. In fact, Keating opened his remarks by decrying how much time and money had been wasted over the "excited fancies of a suspicious old maid. (i.e. Mrs. Amyas.)" The plaintiff (William Gaisford) had his mind poisoned by all this "caddle."[102] For more than three years, Gaisford had spent all his time and a small fortune manufacturing a case that would establish the dishonour of his own wife and the ruin of a respected clergyman. As for the events in London, there was no secret tryst. Everyone in the village knew the Rev. Karr was going to be in the capital. Mrs. Gaisford was in London to visit a dear friend and to pay a call on her husband's relations. When she came to Fladong's hotel, the Rev. Karr, seeing at once "that her visit would be liable to misconstruction, insisted on her leaving." He would get her a cab. He hardly snuck out of the hotel; rather, he left as any gentleman would, 'without any precaution or disguise." He accompanied Mrs. Gaisford in the cab as far as Regents Circus where he dismounted and he had not seen the woman since.

During the time of day the vicar of Berkeley was supposedly debauching Mrs. Gaisford, his movements elsewhere were presented to the jury by a series of alibi witnesses. John Cunningham, who kept a wine shop in Regent Street testified that just after 11 that morning – Rev. Karr, a regular and favoured customer, came to the shop. Cunningham was with a customer so Karr left and returned an hour later. In the interim, the clergyman – as we know, a devoted angler, went in to Bernard's fishing tackle shop off Piccadilly. The owner swore that Mr. Karr was there for most of a diverting hour, which was spent observing the young men in the back making flies and lures. Then, back to Cunningham's, where Karr spent another hour ordering claret. In addition to Cunningham, Boscawen, the cellar-man who (having to interrupt his lunch) fetched the bottles and Ellis, the clerk who made out the dated sales slips also came forward. Lastly, the hall-porter at Mr. Karr's club, the Erechtheum in St. James Square, swore that the vicar had come in about one and remained there until two that afternoon.

If that (overly?) detailed chronology was insufficient, the defense also called Mr. Tilley, the manager of the Roebuck and his barmaid. They both said they would certainly remember a collared clergyman buying drinks in their pub and swore they had never seen the vicar in their boozer. The witness box was then graced by the very proprietor of that "house of ill-fame" in Weymouth Terrace. No doubt used to proceedings of this sort, the witness denied (as was customary) recognizing the lady or gentleman in question. A last witness, for good measure, (pun intended) provided the jury with the exact mileage from Cunningham's wine shop in Regent Street out to the Hackney bawdy house. It was four miles and, so the man swore, it would have been impossible for Mr. Karr to have made a lusty dash thither and back in midday London traffic in the times alleged.

The closing arguments were long and bitterly argued. Keating, going first for Rev. Karr, described the case as a novel one. Mr. Gaisford, the accuser, was posing as the injured husband while he has engaged himself as "a professional agent for the purpose of affording proofs of the dishonour of his wife." He had allied himself with a disreputable figure such as "Mr." Jettings, his London spy:

> There are some thousand cabmen in London, and some thousand cabs, and was it not a very extraordinary coincidence that among the thousands of cabmen, the one who swears to having taken the parties from Henrietta St turned out to be a person whom Mr. Jettings had known from his childhood.

Keating directed the jurymen to study the details of the Rev. Karr's alibi. They were conclusive. In fact, so strong was Mr. Karr's alibi for that day, Keating suggested that the cabman Collins was forced to invent new testimony about what he had supposedly seen through his rooftop door. In desperation, the plaintiff sought to make the eleventh hour claim that even if the clergyman hadn't gone to Weymouth Terrace, he had already debauched Elizabeth in the cab. Collins had never before mentioned that incident. It was a preposterous idea.

> Could they possibly believe that any woman, who was not the most abandoned trull in London, and any gentleman, much less a clergyman, would expose themselves in the noonday in one of the commonest thoroughfares [Holborn] in London?

Keating, before retiring, acknowledged to the jury that his "learned friend" would have much to say about Mr. Gaisford's damages and lost happiness. But think for a moment about the "once lively joyous woman" who was not in court. She no longer enjoys the love and consolation of her children, her life having been ruined by the "jealous delusions" of her unfortunate husband

William Whateley, Gaisford's attorney, opened by stating his appreciation for the fact that, after repeated denials and prevarication, Mr. Karr had, at last, admitted that Elizabeth Gaisford had come to his hotel in London. A married woman, giving no name, meets a gentleman at a hotel. She was seen and identified by numerous witnesses. Soon, in an agitated state, she left. Did the hotel get her a cab? No, it was Mr. Karr, furtively leaving via a side door, who hired the cab. He then rendezvoused with Mrs. Gaisford and they drove away together. Addressing the jury, knowing that many of them were married men, Whateley humbly submitted, "Gentlemen, there's the whole case." How could any husband countenance such questionable conduct on the part of his wife?

The Rev. Karr, Whateley asserted, was a man habituated to the easy morals of Berkeley Castle - the Gloucester jurymen would certainly have gotten the reference. Karr had set out to seduce a gentleman's wife and, all along, the vicar had sneered at the rules of respectable society: from little "liberties" to satin shoes and, inevitably, to a London brothel. Had many of Mr. Gaisford's witnesses been paid? Whateley freely admitted it. These were working people who would be compensated for lost wages. Mr. Gaisford was up against the much greater resources of the Rev. Karr and his Castle allies. The much maligned Jettings, Whateley admitted, was "a man in low life," but such men were necessary as were sheriff's officers, hangmen, and gaolers. Mr. Karr had argued that the evidence of the two cabmen was concocted. But Whateley suggested to the jury that it would have been a lot easier to concoct one story than two. They could have simply claimed that Collins picked them up and took them to Weymouth Terrace. But it happened that there were two cabmen and their stories were for the jurymen to adjudge. As for the defendant's alibi, Whateley thought it was too clever by half. Even with that, it was hardly a complete accounting of the vicar's time. He closed by pleading for these twelve "good men of

Gloucester" to have sympathy for the broken heart of William Gaisford and, by their damages, rebuke the vicar of Berkeley, "this unworthy man who has ruined the peace of this family forever by his heartless conduct."

Pity the jurymen. Who to believe? One side or the other was surely engaged in wholesale perjury. But this was hardly uncommon in a crim. con. action, "notorious for the sickening hypocrisy and barefaced lies that the lawyers had to utter."[103] The trial had been heard by Justice Sir John Patteson – or partly heard as he was nearly deaf but well-respected. Instructing the jury, he stated that it was clear Mrs. Gaisford left Fladong's hotel at just past eleven in the company of the Rev. Mr. Karr. She arrived, alone, at Julia Gaisford's home in Hackney at about two. That journey should never have taken that long.

> If you are satisfied from all the preceding circumstances—that they went to the brothel, you can have no doubt as to the result; but if you are not satisfied that they went to the brothel together, I see no other evidence of any act of adultery at all. For you must remember this is an action for adultery, and not for paying attention to the woman and exciting the suspicions of her husband.

The Gloucester jurymen spent several hours at their task but finally reported they were hopelessly deadlocked. Pressed by the judge to persist, the foreman resisted, "There is no chance of agreement if we're locked up for a month." The jury was dismissed. There was little enthusiasm to repeat the effort in a second trial. The clouded outcome no doubt was more of a blow to Gaisford than the vicar of Berkeley.

Meanwhile, on 23 May, the Dean of Arches issued his ruling. Fust was convinced that yes, Mrs. Gaisford had been in London, she had been at All Souls' church and she had been in Mr. Karr's sitting room at Fladong's Hotel. Remember, in the Arches court, Karr denied all three points.

> If it was not her, Mr. Karr should have told the court who it was. And, as he has not done so, he must be contented to bear the burden of suspicion. If Mr. Karr had any regard for his character and wished to stand high in the opinion of his parishioners, he ought not to have allowed this matter to remain in doubt.

Nonetheless, Fust concluded that there was simply neither the time nor the privacy for actual intercourse to have taken place at Fladong's. But where did Mr. Karr go when he left the hotel in a cab with Mrs. Gaisford? Were the cabmen believable? Fust clearly did not think so, stating that the testimony of Collins and Salmon "by no means satisfied the mind of the court." The credibility of the two drivers had been impeached and the "legal responsibility" for their failings as witnesses rested with the Church. Against the tainted claims of the cabmen, Fust weighed Mr. Karr's alibi which he called "a strong one."

Still, it seemed to be almost with regret that Fust ruled that the charges against the Rev. Karr had not been proven. The Dean had been clearly frustrated with the defendant, who from misplaced gallantry or some other motive, had refused to be completely forthcoming.

> Unfortunately Mr. Karr had himself left the case in very considerable doubt, difficulty and suspicion. He may be innocent of the charges made, yet he had not condescended to give the court any information in his allegation as to how far he proceeded from Fladong's Hotel and having it in his power he would not protect himself from the suspicious circumstances attending his connexion with this lady; he must, therefore, submit to that suspicion which he had brought upon himself.

As his way of demonstrating his dissatisfaction with Karr's [lack of] co-operation, Fust left each side to pay its own legal bills. The Bishop's costs alone had approached £5000 and, presumably, Seton-Karr's were similar. Mr. Karr was re-instated to Berkeley Church but admonished by Mr. Fust to "take care that his household is conducted in a more regular manner in the future." At the very least.

In a matter of a few weeks, the Berkeley solicitor William Gaisford had been dealt two crushing legal defeats. Mr. Karr, meantime, was welcomed back to the town and Castle amid "great rejoicings" from his friends. The *Bristol Times*, ever the enemy of all things Berkeley, decried the outcomes which established the doctrine that "a clergyman may, with impunity, practice any kind of familiarity with the wives of his parishioners, notwithstanding the earnest remonstrances of their husbands to him in private, to the extent even of creating 'great and violent suspicions' of adultery in the minds of the husbands themselves." Gaisford's wrath was unabated; in July he went to his wife's "apartment" to attempt to retrieve furniture and property which he claimed was his before their marriage. There was a scene, some things were broken, and, according to her complaint, he threatened to kill her. The magistrates let him go with a caution and his promise to molest her no more.

The public would move on, of course, to new domestic scandals, some with the added piquancy of a clerical involvement. But the Bishop of Gloucester was left with a monstrous legal bill – the final adjusted accounting came to £4600 pounds - which His Eminence returned to his attorneys as an "indefensible overcharge." The tab was cut to £3600 which the Bishop glumly ordered to be paid so as to finally end what he called a "painful and disgusting topic."

For Rev. Karr, now nearing 40, his raven hair graying, it was a close brush with disgrace. Few would argue with the advice given in one Liverpool newspaper: "It seems highly desirable that every clergyman, fond of female society, and who can well support a wife, ought to marry." Mr. Karr was obviously in need of a wife. In 1855, he married

Anna, widow of Richard Campbell of Auchinbreck.[104] She was made welcome at Berkeley Castle. The Earl died, finally, in 1857 and his old friend, the vicar, handled the funeral in "a solemn and impressive manner."[105]

The Gaisfords were plainly far beyond reconciliation. Elizabeth remained in Bath where she died only a few years later in 1855. The second of the Gaisford sons actually became a clergyman. William Gaisford remarried. He remained a solicitor in Berkeley, even serving a term as mayor, before retiring to Devizes where he died in 1880. His passing was noted with regret at the loss of such an "estimable gentleman."

The Rev. Mr. Karr outlived his tormentor, if only to spite him, perhaps. Karr remained vicar at St. Mary's, Berkeley, until 1871 although he increasingly spent his time in Scotland and left most of his duties to a curate. Karr died at Kippilaw, his home in Roxburghshire, in 1884. The vicar was remembered fondly in Berkeley, for his "eloquence in the pulpit [which] has rarely been excelled ... and as a horseman across country, with his noble patron, he had few equals."[106]

ACKNOWLEDGEMENTS

Sometime about the year 2000, I began compiling notes on Victorian clerical scandals. The database - titled Curious Conduct of the Curate - now numbers several hundred clerics. Inquiries, additions, corrections are always welcome at victorianga@aol.com. Parson Young and the others were selected for their interest and variety of "wrong-doing."

For any Victorian researcher, all acknowledgements must begin with the British Newspaper Archive. With more papers being digitised every year, it is an essential resource. No longer do we have to rely on the London broadsheets alone; newly available Victorian county and local papers are opening new windows. The archive is fee-based but available free in most UK public libraries of substance and at many research libraries in the U.S. and elsewhere. I would also like to thank the staff at the "Newsroom" in the British Library at St. Pancras, as well as the staff at the National Archives in Kew.

Personal information on the individuals in these narratives can be found in the censuses and other records at FamilySearch.com (free) and Ancestry.com (fee-based). The Historical Directories site at the University of Leicester is ever valuable.

I have tried to individually thank those who offered information or assistance in the text or the endnotes. Rupert Courtney-Evans and his wife, Pat, were exceedingly kind to give us a tour of Chipstead and the church. He also shared his research on the village. I appreciate Dr. Neil Clifton's permission to use his recent photo of St. Alban's church in Acton Green. Carol Gingell of Broadland Memories shared her photo of the old Wherry Inn. Rob Sage, clerk to the Batcombe village council, gave me valuable information.

Lastly, I thank my wife, Kathy McGraw, for her unrivaled proof-reading and support.

Previously published by the author:

Blame it on the Devon Vicar (Halsgrove, 2008)
https://www.amazon.com/dp/184114861X

Blame it on the Norfolk Vicar (Halsgrove, 2008)
https://www.amazon.com//dp/1841148628

Clerical Errors - A Victorian Series, Vol. 1 (2016)
https://www.amazon.com//dp/B01CRD2D8O

ENDNOTES

PREFACE
[1] "Scandals of the Time," *South Wales Daily News*, 25 October 1977, 2. (British Newspaper Archive/BNA)
[2] *Manchester Courier*, 9 January 1877 (BNA)
[3] *Reynolds' Newspaper*, 8 May 1870, 4. (BNA)
[4] *Newcastle Chronicle*, 20 May 1865, 4. (BNA)
[5] Matthew Parris, *The Great Unfrocked: Two Thousand Years of Church Scandal*. (1999) xvii.

PARSON YOUNG'S NIGHT OUT
[6] The *St. James Gazette*, February 1884.
[7] Edward Stuart Talbot (1844-1934) Bishop of Rochester (1895-1905). Later Bishop of Southwark and Bishop of Worcester. "He loved being a Bishop."
[8] "Some Little-Known Churches around London," *Ecclesiological Society, Transactions*, Vol. 2, 1890, 102.
[9] The Registers of Wadham College, 1895, 339.
[10] For more, see: http://www.indyrs.co.uk/2011/02/the-reverend-charles-gordon-young-the-birth-of-queens-park-rangers/
[11] "A Village Cricket Match," *The Graphic*, 9 August 1884. (BNA)
[12] Steel & Lyttleton, *Cricket* (1888) 210.
[13] Here I would like to thank Rupert Courtney-Evans, the village historian, who has been so helpful in this area. Rupert and his wife, Pat, gave us a tour of the church and the delightful village. Many of the houses discussed in this article remain in private hands.
[14] Cecil Young Clay Spearing, (b. 1873, Brighton) B.A. 1896, Trinity Hall, Cambridge. Bow, Trinity Hall boat. Solicitor admitted in 1900. Residence: 5 Oxford Terrace, Hyde Park W. The Oxford & Cambridge Yearbook (1904).
[15] "A West-End Night club. A Raid at the Alsatian," *London Daily News*, 21 November 1898, 9. (BNA)
[16] George Cornwallis-West, quoted in Angela Lambert, *Unquiet Souls* (MacMillan, 1984) 6.
[17] This information can be found on the excellent website: http://www.chipsteadvillage.org/News/The-Hamlet-of-Old-Mugswell.
[18] Wentworth Ewing, upon inheriting Shabden from his Uncle

Cattley, took that surname.

[19] Barry Turner, *The Victorian Parson*, (Amberly Publishing, 2015).

[20] J.D. Frost M.A., St. Paul's, Winchmore Hill, Middlesex, "Why I Became an Abstainer," *The Church of England Temperance Magazine*, September 1863.

[21] In 1909, Wentworth Hugh Alexander Ewing Cattley sued for divorce, accusing his wife, Florence Mary Beatrice Cattley (Irish-born) of having committed adultery with Walter Huntingford, an officer on a steamship. Cattley admitted that he and his wife had lived apart for many years and had provided her with a "large sum of money." She called him one day to confess her misconduct and the divorce was undefended. In the 1901 census, Cattley left his marital status open. Mrs. Cattley reported herself to be a "barrister's wife."

[22] Whisky was served at the lunch that followed the meetings. On one occasion, another clergyman, the Rev. Gibson of Charlwood complained that the whisky being provided tasted like "crude oil." Mr. Young added a loud "Hear, Hear," to the debate. The local spirits merchant agreed to upgrade his list.

[23] This possibly refers to the death, by suicide, of the Rev Charles Aubrey Price on 15 September 1897 in Clapham, near London.

[24] Blooming was used as a euphemism for "bloody," like blinking, bleeding, blasted. See Kate Burridge, *Blooming English*, (Cambridge University Press 2004) 209.

[25] (75th canon): No ecclesiastical person shall at any time, other than for their honest necessities, resort to any taverns or alehouses, neither shall they board or lodge in any such places. Furthermore, they shall not give themselves to any base or servile labor, or to drinking or riot, spending their time idly by day or by night, playing at dice, cards, or tables, or any other unlawful games; but at all times convenient they shall hear or read somewhat of the Holy Scriptures, or shall occupy themselves with some other honest study or exercise, always doing the things which shall appertain to honesty, and endeavoring to profit the Church of God; having always in mind that they ought to excel all others in purity of life, and should be examples to the people to live well and Christianly, under pain of ecclesiastical censures, to be inflicted with severity, according to the qualities of their offenses.

(109th canon): If any offend their brethren either by adultery, whoredom, incest, or drunkenness, or by swearing, ribaldry, usury,

and any other uncleanness and wickedness of life, the church wardens or guestmen or sidesmen in their next presentments to their ordinaries, shall faithfully present all and every of the said offenders to the intent that they and every of them may be punished by the severity of the laws according to their deserts; and such notorious offenders shall not be admitted to the Holy Communion till they be reformed.
[26] *Surrey Mirror*, May 24, 1908, 5.

2. A CASE OF HEARTLESS VILLAINY
[27] *The Era*, 1 July 1877, 9. (BNA)
[28] Jenkins, *England's Thousand Best Churches*.
[29] Susanna, Susannah and Susan were used interchangeably but Susanna seems to have been her preferred forename.
[30] Peter Henderson, Archivist, The King's School, Canterbury. Email to the author, 29 December 2016.
[31] Mary Wilson Carpenter, *Health, Medicine, and Society in Victorian England*.
[32] http://www.theatlantic.com/health/archive/2012/10/time-me-gentlemen-the-fastest-surgeon-of-the-19th-century/264065/
[33] Treves: *Scrofula and Its Gland Diseases: An Introduction*. 1882, p. 95.
[34] Gray, *Automatic mechanism, as applied in the construction of artificial limbs in cases of amputation.* (1857) p. 108.
[35] Jenkins, ibid.
[36] "Dr. King on the Treatment of Scrofula," *London Medical Gazette*, (1848) Vol. 6, 105.
[37] 28 March 1857, *Isle of Wight Mercury*, p. 7. (BNA)
[38] James McGrigor Allen, *The Wild Curate*, a Novel. (1887) p. 25.
[39] https://www.genguide.co.uk/source/civil-registration-birth-england-amp-wales/19/
[40] W.H. Ranking, *Researches and observations on the causes of scrofulous diseases, tr., with an intr. and an essay on the treatment of the principal varieties of scrofula.*
[41] Testimony of J.B. Lee, Select Committee on Church Patronage, 11 May 1874.
[42] Larceny Act, 1861 (24 & 25 Vict. c. 96), s. 44
[43] Anthony S. Wohl, ed., *The Victorian Family: Structures and Stresses*, 104.
[44] To have had an abortion was illegal; but the child's birth was

reported. Baby-farming was illegal; it was not illegal to "farm" your child.

[45] Watson's physical description: Complexion florid; hair grey; eyes grey; Height 5'7 ½"; build slender; shape of face oval; peculiarities/marks: scars on throat, chest, back, right groin, and above left knee. Lost his right leg. Rupture on right side. (National Archives, Kew - Calendar of Prisoner Crim 9/23)

[46] Emily was not identified. Watson's younger brother, Henry, married a woman named Emily Mary Bates. It beggar's belief that Watson could have seduced two sisters-in-law. Against that, however, the document suggests that "Emily" was free to marry Watson on his availability.

[47] Clerical Extortioner, *Times of London*. "Who amongst us, listening to the eloquence of his regular Sunday clergyman, has the slightest idea that the clergyman could for a moment have recourse to such "cribs" for his erudition and persuasion?"

[48] National Archives, Kew; Court for Divorce and Matrimonial Causes, J77/199/5262.

[49] William R. Greg, *Why Are Women Redundant?,* London (1869) 5.

[50] *Era* ibid.

[51] "Bankruptcy of a Bucklesham Rector - Embarrassing Financial relations," 17 November 1894, The *Ipswich Journal*, p. 8.

3. A CLERICAL LOTHARIO

[52] W.W. Hutchings, *London Town Past and Present Vol. II* (1909) 915.

[53] Charles N.L. Shaw, "The Creatures of the Night" (1910).

[54] William Le Queux, *The Stretton Street Affair*, (London, 1922) 132.

[55] The hyphen in Cory-Thomas comes and goes. I have chosen to retain it throughout for consistency.

[56] Cory-Thomas' biographical details are taken from *British Columbia from the Earliest Times to the Present*, by E. Scholefield and F. Hovay (1914). Further details can be found at http://www.jwhamil.com/Hamil/Turbie.htm

[57] *Gloucester Journal*, 6 November 1897, 5 (BNA)

[58] *Pall Mall Gazette*, 14 January 1896, 8. (BNA)

[59] Having made a diligent search of the census records and directories for the Acton-Chiswick area in this time period, there are actually two or three "sisters" who meet the criteria: being from a family of three sisters and one brother whose father was dead (or absent) and whose mother died circa 1900. Without confidence,

however, I will withhold their names.

[60] Newnham-Davis, *Dinners and Diners: Where and How to Dine in London* (1899) 69.

[61] Information on Frederick Banks found at Canterburyheritage.blogspot.com, etc. He died in 1894.

[62] Thomas gets a single mention in H.G. McKenzie-Rew, *Records of the Rough Riders (XXth Battalion Imperial Yeomanry.): Boer War, 1899-1902* (1907) 279.

[63] "London Topics of the Week," *New York Times*, February 10, 1901, 4.

[64] Again, at the time of publication, Mrs. T's identity remains unconfirmed.

[65] Mrs. Cory-Thomas was still in London, she did not return to her native New Zealand until 1903.

[66] (Almost heaven?) The local Indians (The Ojibway, now Ojibwe) used the word Ishpeming to mean up, high, or celestial, in the sky. *The Concise Dictionary of the Ojibway Indian Language* is available at http://archive.org.

[67] Joseph Rene Vilatte, born in Paris in 1854. "Wandering" religious figure, literally and spiritually. Ordained an Episcopal minister, he spent a lot of time in the American Midwest, Chicago and Wisconsin, where he certainly met Cory-Thomas. Vilatte received his Archbishop status in 1892 "probably with the blessings of Syriac Orthodox Church." Critics accused Vilatte of "inventing" the "order of the Crown of Thorns." Excommunicated by the Episcopalians, Vilatte founded a cathedral in Green Bay, Wisconsin in 1894 for the American (Old) Catholic Church. For those with an interest, Vilatte's voluminous Wikipedia page is where to begin. He died in 1929.

[68] FreeBMD. England & Wales, Civil Registration Marriage Index, 1837-1915 [database on-line]. Provo, UT, USA: Ancestry.com Operations Inc., 2006.

[69] In Dec 1898, Jessie Jane Phipps, a Sunday School teacher at St. Alban's was charged with damaging a church registry, throwing flowers, etc. She had also threatened both Spink and Cory-Thomas. She was bound over to behave herself for 12 months and left court in the custody of her father and physician. As no father seems to have been present in the home of Miss O and Miss Y, I believe this is a separate (but interesting) case.

[70] A lady giving evidence in a British Court of Justice would be bound to raise her veil on entering the witness box.

[71] Emily Cook, *Highways and Byways in London*, (1903) 291.
[72] According to *Partridge's Dictionary of Slang and Unconventional English*, canoodle was a word created in the 1850's in America but "thoroughly Anglicized" by the London journalist G.A. Sala in 1860's.
[73] Mrs. Isabel Cory-Thomas sailed on the *Rimutaka* from London and arrived in Wellington NZ on 19 Feb 1903. Information courtesy of Sean Doyle at Ancestry.co.uk.
[74] http://www.jwhamil.com/Hamil/Turbie.htm
[75] Spink left Acton to be vicar of St. Stephen's, East Twickenham, in 1905.
[76] "For of this sort are they which creep into houses, and lead captive silly women laden with sins, led away with divers lusts," [2 Timothy 3:6]
[77] "Why are the Clergy Unpopular," *Westminster Review*, 1897, Volume 148, 87.
[78] Taken from Max Beerbohm's review of "*Cousin Kate*" appearing in the *Saturday Review*, 4 July 1903.
[79] Truth, March 7, 1901.

4. I'LL DO FOR DICKY RODGERS
[80] White's *History, Gazetteer & Directory of Suffolk, 1855*; William Alfred Dutt, *The Norfolk Broads*, (1906) 150.
[81] The name of the featured clergyman in this story was alternatively reported in newspaper accounts as Rodgers or Rogers, certainly a common variant. I have chosen to go with Rodgers, citing his official entry in *Crockford's Clerical Directory of 1865*, p. 541.
[82] "The Broads and Rivers of Norfolk & Suffolk," *Blackwood's*. 1879.
[83] *White's Suffolk Directory*, 1874.
[84] Abraham Adderton was a glass & china dealer in the London Road? White's History, Gazetteer and Directory of Suffolk, 1855.
[85] Rodgers' advances and solicitation to commit an unnatural act amounted to indecent assault which was a misdemeanour under the Offences against the Person Act of 1828. The crimes of buggery and/or sodomy (requiring penetration) were a felony which until 1861 was a capital offense. For more, see Cocks, *Nameless Offences: Homosexual Desire in the 19th Century*.
[86] *Cassell's Dictionary of Slang*.
[87] More likely, had Rix gone to the police, the charge would have been simple "indecent behaviour." Without witnesses, "there doesn't seem to have been enough evidence to prove it." E-mail

from Prof. Rictor Norton, author of many books, including *Mother Clap's Molly House: The Gay Subculture in England 1700-1830* (London, 1992).
[88] Dutt, *The Norfolk Broads*
[89] See *Partridge's Dictionary of Slang and Unconventional English* which defines "dicky" as being in bad health, feeling very ill, inferior, sorry, insecure, queer.
[90] Common jurymen received a shilling or eight-pence. More than a few gentlemen of means and spare time supplemented their income by serving on special juries. They were the "guinea pigs." See Oldham, *Trial by Jury: The Seventh Amendment and Anglo-American Special Juries.*

5. THE IRREPROACHABLE MR. KARR
[91] "Berkeley," *The Post Office Directory of Gloucestershire* (1863).
[92] Hope Costley-White, *Mary Cole, Countess of Berkeley* (1973)
[93] *Mary Cole*, op. cit., 198.
[94] In 1836, Charles Edward Bernard, of Clifton, Gloucestershire, claimed that his wife had eloped with Mr. John Seton Karr "from the house of her father in London." Bernard stated: "I feel firmly convinced that the documents will at once show Mr. John Seton Karr, of Christ's College, Cambridge, to have conducted himself in a disgraceful manner, and to be entirely devoid of those feelings by which a gentleman should be actuated."
[95] From Tennyson's *Maud*, "That jeweled mass of millinery, that oiled and curled Assyrian bull, smelling of musk and of insolence." A critic called it one of the crudest lines the poet ever wrote.
[96] *The Musical Times*, (Vol. 40) February 1, 1899, 87.
[97] The family mottoes (translated) were similar and, perhaps, foreshadowing. The Karr motto was "Forward without Fear," while the Setons were likewise heedless, "At whatever risk, yet go Forward."
[98] Cecil B. Hartley, *The Gentlemen's Book of Etiquette and Manual of Politeness*, (2016 reprint) 65.
[99] *Seton-Karr v. Ruther*, at the Gloucester Lent Assizes, 2 April 1850.
[100] There was such a rule under Archbishop Cranmer who, after numerous scandals, decreed in 1552 that "unmarried clergymen were not to retain as housekeepers any women under sixty years of age, except their own near relations." Thomas Buckle, "Fragment on

the Reign of Elizabeth," *Fraser's Magazine*, Vol 76. 145.

[101] Fust died within the year, leaving "eight sons and three daughters, and eighty-three grandchildren."

[102] "Gossip," according to *A Glossary of Dialect & Archaic Words used in the County of Gloucester.* Edited by Lord Moreton (1890).

[103] Wilson, Ben, *The Making of Victorian Values: Decency and Dissent in Britain, 1789-1837* (Penguin, 2007) 150.

[104] They had no children and Mrs. Karr died of cholera in 1866.

[105] Surely, no mention was made of the Earl's other "old friend," his mistress, Mrs. Barker, to whom he left £20,000.

[106] *Western Daily Press* (Bristol), 29 February 1884, 3. (BNA)

Printed in Great Britain
by Amazon